Voices of Prudential and Its People

THE POWER
of A
STORY

Voices of Prudential and Its People

THE POWER of A STORY

Foreword by Arthur F. Ryan
Published by Harcourt, Inc.

Harcourt, Inc.
111 West Jackson Boulevard
Seventh Floor
Chicago, IL 60604

ISBN 0-15-900526-4
Library of Congress Control Number: 2001093690

Produced by The History Factory
www.historyfactory.com

First printing. Printed in U.S.A.
First published 2001

Contents

Foreword

Eighteen seventy-five was an important year. Congress passed the first civil rights legislation. The United States enacted its first trade agreement with the Hawaiian Kingdom. The Kentucky Derby was run for the first time. The first newspaper cartoon strip was printed. And at 812 Broad Street in Newark, New Jersey, the Prudential Friendly Society opened for business.

The beginnings of what would become The Prudential Insurance Company of America were inauspicious. The enterprise started with only $36,000 in the bank. Its chief operating officer was not only a college dropout but also a man with a history of business failures. The company operated out of borrowed offices in the basement of a bank. And almost as soon as the ink on its charter was dry, shareholders started fighting with management.

What was there about Prudential that enabled it to beat the odds against new businesses? I believe it was the importance of the company's founding premise—that working class people should be able to achieve some measure of financial security and peace of mind. Our company began by selling burial insurance to workers so that they could bring dignity to the death of family members without bankrupting themselves.

At the time, it was a revolutionary concept. But it was only the first of many innovations for which Prudential would become known.

If you look inside these pages, you'll learn many interesting facts about our company. Did you know, for example, that throughout our history we've been technical innovators? We were among the first U.S. companies to institute the large-scale use of the telephone. Our actuaries invented keypunch machines. Our managers invented an early form of the copy machine. And we started using computers in 1935 in collaboration with a little-known company called International Business Machines. That tradition of technological innovation is still alive today with our LaunchPad program for agents and our linkage with Palm VII organizers.

We were also one of the first companies to recognize the importance of operating in many markets. Our international operations began in 1909, when we opened an office in Canada. More recently, our groundbreaking work in Japan, which started in 1981, ran against the counsel of many "experts" who told us that the American method of selling insurance would never be accepted in that country. We proved them wrong in Japan and in many other countries since, bringing with us not only our professional sales force but also our long-standing tradition of being involved in the communities where we do business.

Through the years, we also have been among the pacesetters for our industry. When it became apparent that the interests of our stakeholders were not meshing with the interests of our customers, we changed from a stock company to a mutual company in 1913. Decades later, at the start of the revolution in financial services, we were among the first insurance companies to acquire other financial institutions with our purchase in 1981 of Bache Halsey Stuart Shields (now Prudential Securities Inc.).

Our visionary response to an evolving world is taking place as I write. When we finished compiling this book, we were exploring whether we should demutualize. As we go to print, we're much further along in that process—we're learning from our policyholders whether they believe their interests will best be served by a new, publicly held company—Prudential Financial.

We have a long history of innovation, but I don't believe it is the primary reason for Prudential's 125 years of achievement and success. No, we've been around this long because we keep our promises. Prudential people have worked hard, with dedication and foresight, to help our customers achieve financial security and peace of mind, treating each customer with dignity and respect and offering excellent service.
In other words, we do the right work in the right way to produce the right results.

In my tenure with the company, I've found that the best way to learn the real story of Prudential is from my colleagues. The people of Prudential have created its history, and I'm proud that *The Power of a Story* is an oral history—it shows us Prudential's heritage as it has been nurtured each day in our relationships with our clients, with our communities and with each other.

I hope you enjoy your exploration of Prudential's legacy as much as I have.
Happy birthday, Prudential!

Arthur F. Ryan
Chairman and Chief Executive Officer
June, 2001

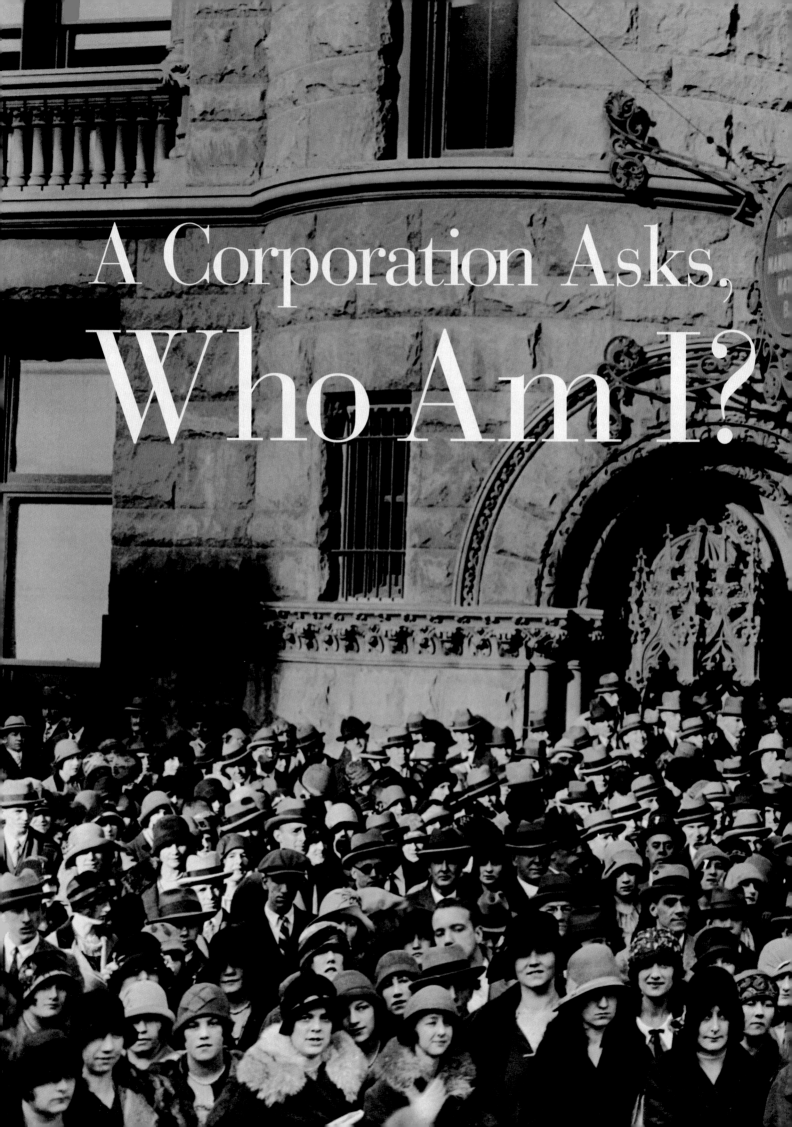

A Corporation Asks, Who Am I?

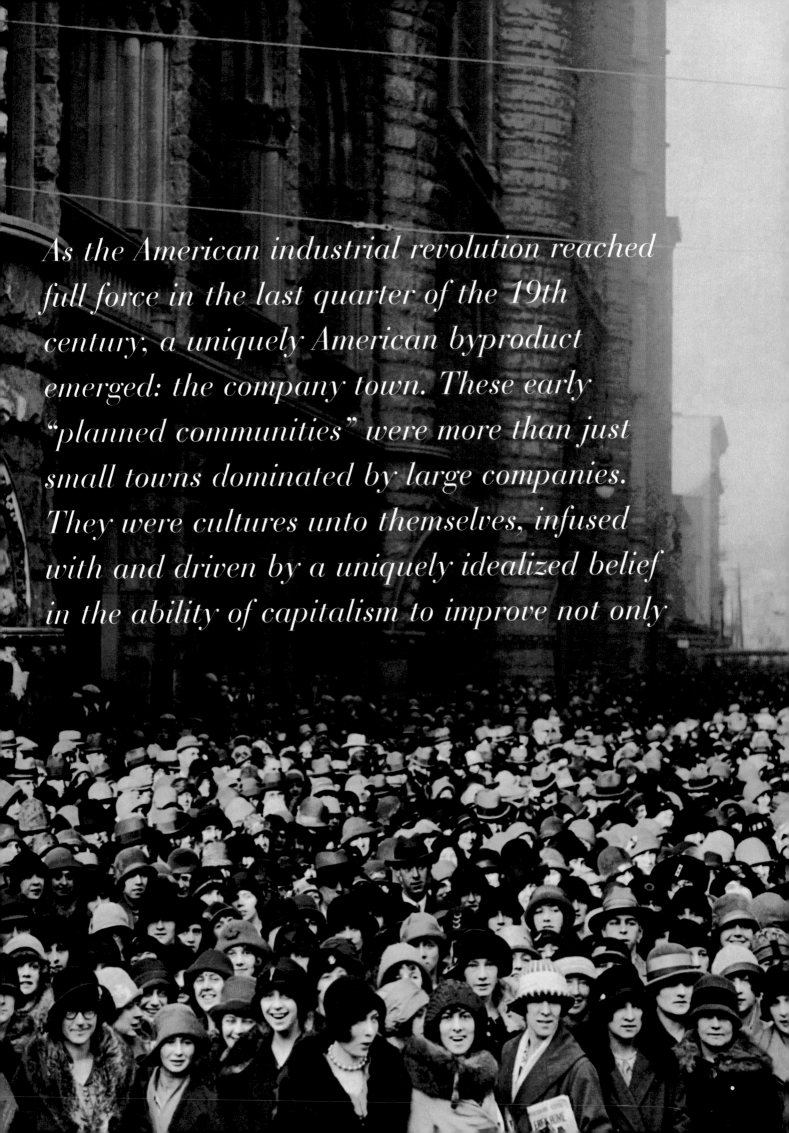

As the American industrial revolution reached full force in the last quarter of the 19th century, a uniquely American byproduct emerged: the company town. These early "planned communities" were more than just small towns dominated by large companies. They were cultures unto themselves, infused with and driven by a uniquely idealized belief in the ability of capitalism to improve not only

material well-being but citizenship, character
and morality as well.

   After World War I, as immigration subsided
and the automobile and mass transit allowed
workers greater mobility, those self-contained
"company towns" slowly disappeared. In the
interest of morale and productivity, however,
corporate leaders remained committed to
developing a work force whose attachment
to the job transcended weekly paychecks.

PRECEDING PAGE: EMPLOYEES GATHER IN THE "PRU CANYON," THE SPACE BETWEEN THE
PRUDENTIAL MAIN AND NORTH BUILDINGS, OCTOBER 24, 1925. ABOVE: THE "PLEASURE
CLUB," 1884. OPPOSITE (CLOCKWISE): (FROM LEFT) RICHARD BENNETT, NEWARK FIREMAN;
JOHN CAULFIELD, NEWARK FIRE DIRECTOR AND STATE SENATOR; JERRY TERAPOKIA AND
DORIS HOUSTON OF PRUDENTIAL, 1980; A TEAM OF SCHO VOLUNTEERS IN THE COMPANY'S
RECORDS MANAGEMENT CENTER, 1999; EMPLOYEES ON EXCURSION DAY, JULY 22, 1937.

THE ATHLETIC ASSOCIATION
of the PRUDENTIAL INSURANCE COMPANY
JOINS WITH THE NEWARK FIRE DEPT.
IN THE CHRISTMAS TOY DRIVE

New developments—particularly internal company publications—took the place of planned communities. Some companies established a local identity by creating a different magazine for each mill or factory. Company newspapers not only shared news about the workplace, they also listed social and recreational events, items for sale and the latest gossip. After work, many businesses sponsored athletic teams as well as company outings and picnics.

Prudential has succeeded over its 125 years in creating its own corporate culture: a "city within a city." Lifelong friendships developed

OPPOSITE (TOP): THE COMPANY'S FIRST BASKETBALL COURT, ON THE 13TH FLOOR OF THE NORTH BUILDING, 1919. OPPOSITE (BOTTOM): PRUDENTIAL INSURANCE COMPANY ATHLETIC ASSOCIATION MEMBERS AT NEWARK AIRPORT, 1955. ABOVE (FROM LEFT): AGENT'S PRUDENTIAL, JULY 1891; THE PRU ECHO, JANUARY 1953; THE PICA NEWS, APRIL 21, 1955.

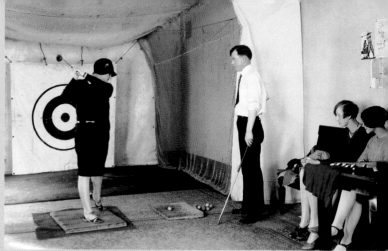

as co-workers shared their daily lives—on
and off the job—and it was not uncommon to
have three generations of families working at
Prudential. For most of its history, the company
provided a free lunch for employees in its larger
offices. Prudential also organized athletic leagues,
fashion shows and excursions. For many summers
before and after World War II, Prudential's
Newark employees and their families boarded

a special train to Asbury Park, New Jersey, where they enjoyed a day of sand and surf.

At the beginning of the 21st century, when the primary focus of corporations appears to be the bottom line, the cultural element of corporate life might seem seriously threatened. While personal taste as well as economic

OPPOSITE (CLOCKWISE): A CHRISTMAS CELEBRATION IN THE PRESS ROOM, 1923; A COMPANY-SPONSORED GOLF CLINIC, ca. 1920s; AN ATHLETIC ASSOCIATION TRIP TO THE POCONOS, PENNSYLVANIA, ca. 1950. *ABOVE:* A TREASURE HUNT ON THE BEACH AT ASBURY PARK, NEW JERSEY, 1967.

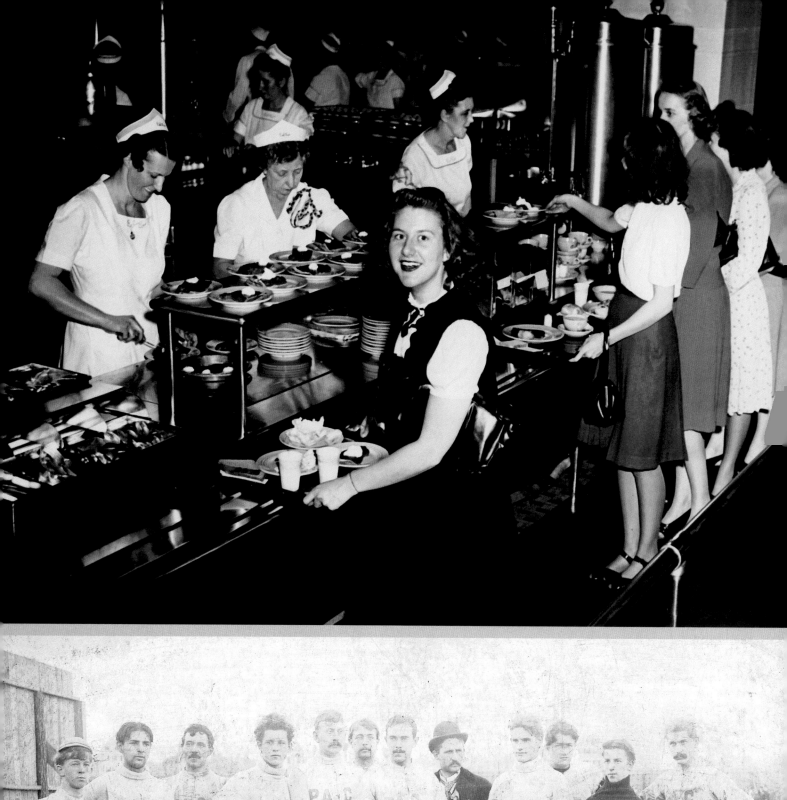

pressures and competition will never allow the kind of paternalistic, all-encompassing communality of the industrial revolution, companies such as Prudential recognize what those early culture-builders knew more than a century ago: A company's greatest asset is its people. Creating corporate culture and identity in the 21st century will be a trickier and subtler business, but it perhaps will be more important than ever.

OPPOSITE (TOP): THE WASHINGTON STREET BUILDING CAFETERIA, ca. 1945. *OPPOSITE (BOTTOM):* MEMBERS OF THE ORDINARY AND INDUSTRIAL FOOTBALL SQUADS, THE COMPANY'S FIRST TEAMS, ca. 1894. *ABOVE:* (FROM LEFT) LILLIAN CALDWELL, VIVIAN WYATT, KATHY GREGOWITZ AND CAMILLE MAYERSKI WITH A 14,000 POUND PIECE OF THE ROCK OF GIBRALTAR AT THE NEW PROVIDENCE, NEW JERSEY, OFFICE, 1981.

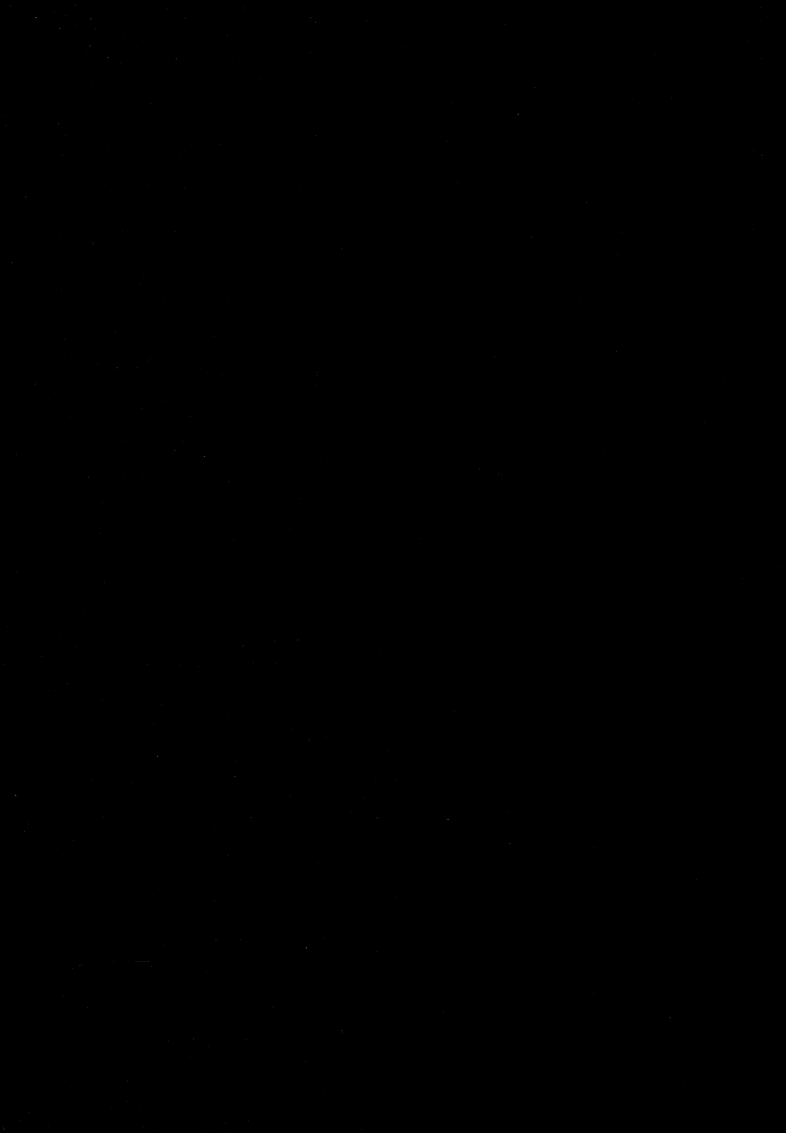

Building a Foundation

The First 100 Years of Prudential

"A Belief Before It Was a Business"

More than a quarter-century ago, a *Fortune* magazine article described Prudential as a "kind of universal power plant, vast of maw and spout." But more remarkable than the company's size, sensed the author, was its continued steadfastness of purpose: At Prudential, life insurance "was a belief before it was a business."

Before Prudential, there was little mass-distributed life insurance in America, at least not as we know it today. "Industrial insurance" (as life insurance for wage earners was called at that time) had its roots in 19th-century England. This kind of insurance, whose premiums were low and paid weekly, was created to serve the expanding and always financially strapped working class. On the other side of the Atlantic, however, the only people before 1875 who could afford life (then called "ordinary") insurance were those who already enjoyed a level of affluence. Working stiffs, it was assumed, couldn't be trusted to volunteer the payments and probably wouldn't have the discipline to save up for them anyway. As Frederick Hoffman explained it in his 1900 history of Prudential, "Industrial insurance is practically mass insurance, while Ordinary insurance is, in a measure, class insurance."

Before you could offer insurance to the workingman, you first had to believe in him. And that wasn't easy. In the early 1860s, Elizur Wright, the commissioner of insurance for Massachusetts and the foremost American insurance expert, delivered a report to that state's legislature, opining that industrial insurance was not suitable for the United States. (Among his arguments was the belief—common to the wealthy—that if the lower classes were allowed to insure their children, they would be tempted to murder them for the money.) Most of those who thought about the matter at all took Wright's position as final and definitive.

However, the working class had a great need for life insurance. A large majority of Americans of this period were, by any standards, poor. After feeding and sheltering their often large families, workingmen faced a real fear of dying without even enough money for the decent disposition of their remains. The company's history, *Fifty Years of The Prudential*, put the matter quite succinctly: "Few of our more intelligent people, especially those in the middle or upper economic classes, realize the horror and apprehension that the mere idea of a pauper burial inspires in the hearts of all people."

A 1906 Bureau of Labor bulletin described the situation: "Figures show that insurance is held in high esteem, but they do not tell how great a moral force it is in the lives of the poor. How is it that people who are barely holding body and soul together, and who are so sorely pressed by the demands of the present, will surrender a part of the income … to the purchase of a benefit that can accrue only in the future? The sentiment which prompts the poor to invest in insurance is akin to piety; if death should come into the family they want the household to be protected from

Dryden disputed the presumption that working people lacked the character and habits that would permit them to pay for insurance.

harsh and profane influence and they want the departed one to receive a decent burial."

Yet an 1875 study by the Massachusetts Bureau of Labor Statistics found that of 397 workingmen's families, only one had any insurance protection whatsoever. When death darkened the door, it was time to pass the hat. Otherwise, what awaited the worker at the end of his labors was the final indignity of an unnamed plot in a potter's field.

This problem piqued the interest of John Fairfield Dryden. Born in 1839 in Maine, the son of a farmer and odd-jobber, his own upbringing sensitized him to the troubles common to all working-class families. Somehow, between occasional stints in the shops and mills of Worcester, Massachusetts, where the family settled for some years, he received a good education and admission to Yale. Never physically robust, he left Yale after his second year, reportedly because of poor health.

But while still in college, perhaps because of his struggle to simply make do while surrounded by so many young men of privilege, young Dryden became obsessed with the idea of industrial insurance. Dryden studied Elizur Wright's report and disagreed, if then only on instinct, with its findings. In 1865, two years after leaving Yale, he set out to educate himself on the intricacies of industrial insurance, which had established by this time a firm foothold in England. If it could work in England, he felt, why not in America?

Dryden had embarked upon a lifetime in the insurance business—a lifetime (after several false starts) spent largely at the helm of

THE DRYDEN FAMILY HOME IN TEMPLE HILLS, MAINE, ca. 1840s. WHEN JOHN F. DRYDEN WAS 8, HIS FATHER MOVED THE FAMILY FROM MAINE TO MASSACHUSETTS TO BEGIN WORK AS A MACHINIST.

what would become The Prudential Insurance Company of America.

Tough Times

Leaving New Haven, Dryden and his new wife moved to the Midwest, where he toiled in several insurance jobs without making much headway. The long recession following the Civil War might have hampered his professional progress, but for whatever reasons, Dryden and his family headed back East in 1867, leaving behind some unpaid debt.

Life wasn't much better in New York City. He moved from job to job, changing addresses three times in the next three years. But Dryden continued to nurture his obsession, reading everything he could about industrial insurance. His greatest resources were the many articles printed at the time in praise of the Prudential Assurance Company of Great Britain, which began offering industrial insurance upon its founding in 1848.

The more he read, the stronger Dryden's convictions grew. Moreover, being of the working class himself, Dryden disputed the presumption that working people lacked the character and habits that would permit them to pay for insurance. Indeed, he believed, owning an industrial policy would reinforce those very tendencies. (The first Prudential prospectus, almost surely penned by Dryden himself, reflected this sentiment: "A membership in The Prudential will induce prudence and economy, and become the foundation of good habits.")

And, surely, the fact didn't escape him that where there's a need, and even modest wherewithal, there's a market.

Meanwhile, Dryden languished in an obscure Brooklyn insurance office until 1873. That year, when he moved his family to Newark, the Drydens were on the edge of poverty. He was, by this time, 34 years old and, for all his zeal and commitment, had already accrued a string of failures.

What brought him to Newark, nobody knows. He knew no one. His family took residence in a less-than-opulent rooming house, and prospects seemed no brighter than before. He soon found work at The Widows and Orphans Friendly Society, which wrote small ordinary insurance policies on a group basis. As was probably his habit, Dryden bombarded Allen Bassett, the society's proprietor, with his knowledge of industrial insurance and soon convinced him that offering such insurance to Newark's factory workers was a viable and potentially lucrative idea.

The first (and easiest) thing to change was the name of the company, which became, in 1875, The Prudential Friendly Society. While the not inconsiderable task of raising start-up money remained, Dryden must have experienced what for him was a rare emotion: optimism. Bassett knew people with the funds that would allow Dryden to realize his vision. For example, Bassett introduced Dryden to Dr. Leslie D. Ward, who, though at first skeptical and dismissive, subscribed for $1,000 worth of stock and, most importantly, spread the word among his wealthy Newark friends. Within a few weeks, the determined Dryden had raised the necessary $6,000 in reserve capital necessary to commence this new enterprise, but it would take the rest of

ALLEN BASSETT WAS ELECTED DIRECTOR AND FIRST PRESIDENT OF THE PRUDENTIAL FRIENDLY SOCIETY ON OCTOBER 13, 1875. IN JUST SIX MONTHS, THE COMPANY HAD 5,000 POLICIES IN FORCE.

1875 to raise the $30,000 in pledged capital necessary to begin writing insurance.

In mid-October, the newly formed board of directors elected Allen Bassett president and John Dryden secretary. Twenty-four of Newark's business and professional elite buttressed the young Prudential as its principal stockholders. The *Newark Register* gushed, "One of the most gratifying facts connected with this society is its strength and security. [The Prudential] may be said to be founded upon a rock." Rock, indeed.

Refining the Concept

Dryden must have felt like an uncaged bird. Finally, what had been confined to his zealous imagination was now a desk-and-blotter reality. He wasted no time. Speaking in front of assembled factory workers (most often at plants owned by members of the board), he sold the idea of industrial insurance, or to put it more directly, he sold the policies themselves. In fact, by the end of 1875, Prudential had sold 284 policies, and a little more than six months after opening its doors, Prudential had 5,000 policies in force. The company was on its way.

That's not to say that Prudential didn't have some problems in its early years. A first-anniversary audit indicated that, despite issuing more than 7,000 policies, Prudential was more than $1,500 in debt. Something had to be done. Nothing indicates that anyone seriously entertained the idea of closing Prudential's doors. Board members had faith in Dryden and his ideas, which, they determined, simply required adjustment. The directors decided that the company needed further benefit of British Prudential's experience; someone should be sent to London to examine its operations. The man for the job was, quite naturally, Dryden himself.

Prudential's secretary returned from London with a much sharper comprehension of the nuts and bolts of the industrial insurance business. Dryden shared his discoveries with the board, and with its enthusiastic approval and encouragement, those revelations became policy. Rates were raised, actuarial tables altered and bookkeeping practices and standardized forms simplified.

It is worth noting that Dryden didn't merely imitate British Prudential. In fact, he resisted the suggestion that he should simply adopt the British rates. Americans, he said, had longer life spans, and the reserves could be invested at higher returns than were possible in England. His Prudential was to be an American experiment, not an imitation of the British company.

To everyone's relief, Dryden's fine-tuning did the trick. The ledger began to show more black than red. Reflecting an increased confidence, the company's name was changed in 1877 to The Prudential Insurance Company of America.

The new name represented hope rather than

THE ELIZABETH, NEW JERSEY, BRANCH OFFICE AS IT APPEARED IN MAY 1889, A DECADE AFTER OPENING. PRUDENTIAL OPENED ITS FIRST BRANCH OFFICE IN PATERSON, NEW JERSEY, IN APRIL 1878.

reality. The company was still, in essence, The Prudential Insurance Company of Newark, but it was ready to expand.

Early Growth

Bassett and Dryden chose Paterson, New Jersey, another city with abundant industry, for their initial foray out of Newark. Paterson soon provided considerable business, and branches in Jersey City, Elizabeth and Camden followed.

Two characteristics contributed greatly to the company's early success, characteristics that would serve the company over its entire history. The first was a basic and practical parsimoniousness. For example, discarded envelopes were used for scratch paper, and the clerks were urged to write fine, small characters to reduce the amount of paper they used.

Secondly, even in its infancy, Prudential enjoyed a reputation for fair business practices and extraordinary service to its customers. On July 6, 1878, for instance, the *Paterson Guardian* reported, "The fact that six persons died in one day—that their friends took their policies to the company's office and got the money for them, all in 24 hours—is something which has never been seen in this or any other city of this country before." As word got out, profits increased. Before the company's second anniversary, Prudential had

---

'One of the most gratifying facts connected with this society is its strength and security. [The Prudential] may be said to be founded upon a rock.'

more than 10,000 policies in force and was selling roughly 500 more each week. Word of mouth—aided by Dryden and Bassett's insistence upon dealing directly with potential customers—accounted for the large majority of those policies.

Changes in Leadership

The desire to expand into Pennsylvania and New York prompted Prudential's first in-house ruckus. Expansion required raising additional capital, which, under Bassett's leadership, did not seem forthcoming. Although the minutes of the May 1879 board meeting are not explicit, we do know that the meeting began on the topic of expansion and ended with Bassett's resignation. History would see the change of leadership as a smart move. Prudential needed more committed and focused leadership at this crucial moment than Allen Bassett could provide. (The company, however, had not seen the last of Mr. Bassett. He soon became a major player—for the other side—in Prudential's early street fights with its soon-to-be rival, Metropolitan Life.)

With Bassett out, Dryden might have seemed the logical successor. But Dryden, a man of small means at the time of the company's founding, continued to accept only a modest salary. Deference, during this period, was paid to money over brains and vision. Newark's capitalists had made the establishment of Prudential possible, and they would choose from among their own.

Indeed, as Prudential's second president, they elected Noah Blanchard, a prominent Newark businessman who owned a large

IN 1879, NOAH BLANCHARD BECAME PRUDENTIAL'S SECOND PRESIDENT. BLANCHARD EMPHASIZED THAT INSURANCE SERVED AS VALUABLE PROTECTION FOR FAMILIES OF SMALL MEANS.

tannery. (Incidentally, Blanchard was hardly a classic patrician. His clothes consistently reeked of his tannery. As one early Prudential employee lamented, "As soon as he entered the premises, you could, without looking up, tell by the smell that the president had arrived; in fact, if the wind was right, you could detect that he was on his way.")

Dryden wouldn't see the presidency of the company for another two years, and even then, the ascendancy would be ugly. In 1881, Blanchard died, and yet again, Dryden was not the presumptive heir to the corner office. More boardroom roughhousing ensued. Only through the stubborn support of an original board member, Dr. Leslie D. Ward, did Dryden gain election to the presidency, and, then, by a margin of just one vote.

Growing Pains

While Prudential was undergoing these early leadership adjustments, other external events were taking place that would define the company for years to come. Increasingly confident, Prudential was ready to move beyond the Jersey border. Yet while New York and Philadelphia represented increased opportunity, they also meant increased competition, particularly from the Metropolitan Life Insurance Company, Prudential's slightly older and more patrician cousin across the Hudson.

These weren't easy times to be patrician, however. Prior to 1879, the Met offered only ordinary life policies, but its wealthier clientele had been hit hard by an economic depression that had already lasted six years. The ordinary market had virtually collapsed, and to stem the bleeding, the Met had launched itself fervently into industrial insurance. There it ran headlong into the Prudential, which was now, the Met felt, invading its territory.

The Met went after the industrial market with extraordinary vehemence, quickly expanding into nine states. This was at the same time (1879) that Prudential was establishing beachheads in New York and Philadelphia. Each company had a lot resting on wrenching every dime from its new territories.

It's impossible to determine who lobbed the first grenade, or even at times to determine who the grenadiers were. For instance, no one knows quite what or who prompted this inflammatory commentary in one New York newspaper: "It may be known to some of our readers that a small, one-horse insurance company, with its headquarters at Newark, New Jersey, is actually endeavoring to scoop in a harvest of victims in this city and state. With the grandiloquence that naturally arises from ignorance and presumption, it baptized itself the Prudential, after the great industrial assurance society of that name in England. ... On the 31st day of July 1879 its agents crossed the

AGENT ADAM FOREMAN IN A NEW YORK DISTRICT OFFICE, ca. 1888. PRUDENTIAL'S MOVE INTO THE NEW YORK MARKET CREATED FIERCE COMPETITION WITH AREA COMPANIES.

Hudson River and invaded this city like a microscopic pestilence of an army of worms or hornets."

Accusations of agent filching, as well as organizational and financial instability, flew back and forth. Some Prudential agents did jump to the Met and, probably vice versa. In 1881, Allen Bassett himself popped up as the Met's head of operations in northern New Jersey, bent, presumably, on revenge. After Bassett's appointment became known, both sides took the gloves off and went bare-knuckled, for several years, in a series of bushwhacks and skirmishes never before witnessed in a rather staid industry.

Ultimately, cooler heads—those atop the shoulders of John Dryden and Messrs. Knapp and Hegeman, who ran the Met—prevailed. To continue this interstate unseemliness, they felt, would ultimately destroy both companies and degrade the industry itself. The chiefs of the warring tribes met in New York City and agreed to keep their field forces on a short leash. While a healthy competition prevails to this day, open bloodshed became a thing of the past.

A Big New Home

A mere three years after opening its doors, Prudential's success required more room than its

While Prudential was undergoing early leadership adjustments, other external events were taking place that would define the company for years to come.

original basement office at 812 Broad Street could accommodate. In 1878, the company moved to the Centennial Building on Market Street, where its square footage increased threefold. By its 10th anniversary in 1885 — now boasting more than a million dollars in assets as well as a million industrial policies in force — the company moved again, this time to the Jube Building at 878-880 Broad Street.

Within five years, even that building would prove inadequate. Dryden, now firmly established at the top of the letterhead, felt Prudential deserved its own edifice. The construction of The Prudential Building would not only reduce the likelihood of another disruptive move but, more importantly, would also symbolize the company's stability and prosperity. The new headquarters formally opened on December 2, 1892, and for seven decades, through two world wars and the Great Depression, this grand dame would preside over a vast financial empire. Metaphorically, at least.

The Prudential Building proved a splendid home but didn't quite fulfill its expectations. With the addition of new and popular offerings in ordinary insurance — the company was soon selling more than 2,000 ordinary policies a year — and the general growth in Prudential's name and reputation, further expansion was soon necessary. Within the next eight years, four annexes were added nearby.

Furthermore, The Prudential Building, for all its grandeur, didn't quite hit the mark as a symbol of the company. Prudential's advertising

OPENED IN 1892, THE COMPANY'S NEW HEADQUARTERS FEATURED HOT AND COLD RUNNING WATER, ELECTRIC WIRING THROUGHOUT AND FIVE HYDRAULIC ELEVATORS THAT MOVED 500 FEET A MINUTE.

tried to link the edifice to the company's image as a "Tower of Strength," but somehow it didn't draw the desired response. The company needed another symbol. Some formidable brainstorming ensued, from which one of the most recognizable commercial icons in the world arose: the Rock.

To Washington — and Beyond

By the 1890s, Prudential and, indeed, the entire American insurance industry had become "Big Business" at precisely the time when Progressive Americans were casting a skeptical eye upon such monolithic enterprises.

Prudential, like most large insurance companies, had by this time entered into elaborate financial relationships with banks and related businesses, and this type of agreement attracted the greatest public scrutiny. While Prudential had done nothing illegal, the company, along with the "Big Three" (Equitable, New York Life and Mutual Life), was forced to testify before New York state's Armstrong Commission. Dryden, by this time a U.S. senator, volunteered to appear before the commission on December 12, 1905. It was a bravura performance. Dryden (apparently alone among the insurance executives who testified) showed a fingertip command of his business and explained its workings and principles proudly and without defensiveness.

Altogether, it was a tour de force. Dryden personally managed to rehabilitate not only the public standing of his own company but also, to some extent, the industry as a whole. Ultimately, as a result of such scrutiny, the industry wisely began to disentangle itself from questionable alliances and, if anything, gained in reputation. Thanks to the able and elegant testimony of John Dryden, Prudential weathered the ordeal with dignity.

This same anti-big business sentiment directly affected John Dryden's political career. By 1902, Prudential's president was well connected within New Jersey Republican circles and he won a seat in the U.S. Senate. In part, because he retained all his business responsibilities while a senator and additionally because of the investigations recounted above, Dryden's senatorial tenure was, while respectable, unremarkable. When the time came for proposing his renomination in 1906, the party was split between old-liners and reformists. The latter group naturally opposed Dryden as a member of the conservative establishment. Amidst the ruckus, Dryden, disappointed but gracious, withdrew from the race, pleading ill health.

While sickness might have provided a convenient excuse for extricating Dryden from an unsavory political mess, it wasn't far from the truth. Dryden had never enjoyed a vigorous constitution, and the end of the decade found him feeling like an old man. Dr. Leslie Ward—Dryden's friend, colleague and early champion—

MEMBERS OF THE SAN FRANCISCO BRANCH OFFICE CREATED A MEMORIAL FOR THE COMPANY'S FOUNDER UPON HIS DEATH IN NOVEMBER 1911.

died in 1910, and with his passing, Dryden found himself the last surviving figure among the daring men who founded Prudential. The world was changing and, with early intimations of mutualization, so would Prudential—so would its leadership.

In the book *From Three Cents a Week ...*, William Carr described Dryden's last days: "On Saturday, November 18, 1911, John Dryden was operated on in his home at 1020 Broad Street in Newark, so that gallstones could be removed. He was said to be 'doing well,' but within another day or two the doctors were expressing 'little hope.' Pneumonia had set in. Late on the afternoon of Friday, November 24, death came to the man whom *The New York Times* described the next morning as the 'Father of Industrial Insurance.'"

Yes, Dryden was an innovator and a visionary, but perhaps Dryden's most fitting epitaph came from Carr: "He was tough. He had to be, in a time when the financial world was like a wild, lawless frontier. Dryden was fiercely independent. At a time when many other life insurance companies fell under the domination of one Wall Street giant or another, he kept the Prudential a thing apart. ... He would make alliances—when it benefited the Pru—with various interests, but in the end the Pru always

The company needed another symbol. Some formidable brainstorming ensued, from which one of the most recognizable commercial icons in the world arose: the Rock.

stood alone, representing no interests but its policyholders."

It is also worthwhile to note, as did Carr, that at the time of Dryden's death, Prudential's assets amounted to more than a quarter-billion dollars—"all of it built up from his dream and a few thousand dollars invested by businessmen whom he and Dr. Ward had converted to the cause. ... He had seen how to satisfy a social need, he had struggled against long odds to bring his dream to realization and he had reaped the rewards. After his death *The New York Times* estimated his fortune at $50,000,000 — not much less than the $68,000,000 left by J.P. Morgan on his death two years later. Morgan led the honorary pallbearers at Dryden's funeral."

Not bad for a fellow described soon after his arrival in Newark as "unknown and penniless."

Forrest Dryden and Mutualization

John Dryden's son, Forrest Fairchild Dryden, had been groomed for some years for Prudential's presidency. As a boy, he had worked part time in the home office, and after graduation from Phillips Academy in 1882 he joined the Prudential full time as a clerk. His clerk's chair was hardly warm before the elder Dryden placed the career ladder before him and pointed upward. Eight years after joining the company, he was a member of the board, and, a year after that, third vice president. In 1906, he was named second vice president, in 1911, vice president, and, in January 1912, he succeeded his deceased father as president of Prudential.

While it is tempting to envy such a

FORREST F. DRYDEN, WITH HIS FATHER JOHN F. DRYDEN IN 1906. THE YOUNGER DRYDEN JOINED THE COMPANY IN 1882 AT THE AGE OF EIGHTEEN AND BECAME ITS PRESIDENT IN 1912.

privileged ascension, the younger Dryden was taking the reins at a difficult time.

For almost a generation, shareholders had grumbled that they weren't receiving their proper share of the company's surplus earnings. To the shareholders, surplus earnings looked like withheld dividends. Policyholders, they argued, were given undue preference. By 1910, the matter had come to a head. In his final months with the company, John Dryden had argued that the issue boiled down to who would control the mission and character of the company, and naturally, Dryden felt strongly that Prudential's customers would be best served by maintaining the status quo. Shortly before his death, a compromise was reached that was unsatisfactory to both sides. (An accompanying lawsuit brought by the heirs of Prudential's second president, Noah Blanchard, was resolved —not in Prudential's favor—in 1912.)

Furthermore, back in 1902, Prudential had entered a complicated stockholder relationship with Fidelity Trust Bank, an arrangement that Dryden had engineered to diminish the power of his (now disgruntled) shareholders. Technically, Fidelity and Prudential both owned sufficient stock to control the fate of the other, but during John Dryden's tenure, a gentlemen's agreement held that each company would honor the integrity of the other. With the elder Dryden's passing, the leaders of Fidelity no longer respected the agreement and moved to take control of Prudential's board of directors and, with it, the company's future. A fracas ensued, each side maneuvering with all the skill for which lawyers and boards of directors are so famous. In a last-minute flanking tactic master-minded by the astute Richard Lindabury, Prudential's chief counsel, Fidelity was cornered.

According to Earl Chapin May's 1950 history of the company, *The Prudential: A Story of Human Security*, Lindabury put the matter to Forrest Dryden in no uncertain terms: "The only way to end this clamor and destroy this threat is finally and irrevocably to take the company out of the hands of those who endanger it." Forrest Dryden agreed, and Fidelity had no choice but to go along. In 1912, both sides realized that further hostility would lead nowhere and agreed that the solution was to mutualize the Prudential. Mutualization became a legal reality a year later.

Mutualization ensured the company's independence from any future outside interference. But the company's transformation into a mutual life insurance company—owned and controlled exclusively by policyholders—was no easy matter. Repurchasing stock, particularly from stockholders not altogether pleased with their lot, remained a tricky and time-consuming business. The majority of stockholders sold their shares back to Prudential in 1915, and the company operated as a mutual company from that time onward, but it would take another 30 years

JOHN F. DRYDEN HIRED RICHARD LINDABURY AS CHIEF COUNSEL AFTER HE SUCCESSFULLY REPRESENTED PRUDENTIAL'S MINORITY STOCKHOLDERS IN 1902, PREVENTING A MERGER WITH FIDELITY TRUST.

before all of Prudential's shares were owned by the company itself.

Prudential's renewed independence through mutualization was Forrest Dryden's greatest accomplishment as president. "As a result of this practical completion of mutualization," May wrote, "Prudential at the end of 1915 was able to apportion about $4,000,000 more to its dividends to policyholders."

However, Forrest Dryden would begin and end his tenure as Prudential's president with the company under a legal cloud. The investigation of financial institutions had seemingly become the government's favorite indoor sport. This time, instigated by an acute postwar housing shortage, the inquiry focused on home mortgages, or what the government perceived as the deliberate and predetermined shortage of these mortgages. New York's newly appointed Lockwood Committee seemed hell-bent on proving that Prudential and other companies were restricting mortgage funds and, by doing so, discouraging the construction and ownership of homes.

While evidence suggests that the committee specialized in political showcasing, it most certainly drew blood. This time, Prudential, and Forrest Dryden in particular, did not fare well.

'*He had seen how to satisfy a social need, he had struggled against long odds to bring his dream to realization and he had reaped the rewards.*'

The brilliant Richard Lindabury succeeded in using state-produced research to prove that Prudential's mutualization was genuine and forthright, but as for other financial involvements —including lingering Fidelity Trust entanglements as well as mortgage practices—Prudential and Dryden stood on less solid ground. To put it bluntly, Forrest Dryden's performance was uninspiring. Under questioning, he didn't seem to have much of an understanding of the workings of his own company. And despite Lindabury's efforts, there was little evidence to countermand Dryden's poor showing.

As soon as possible, Dryden took a leave of absence and let the remaining Prudential leadership clean house. Shortly before he was to return, Forrest Dryden resigned. He must have walked away in August 1922 feeling that he'd let down both Prudential and his esteemed father.

EMPLOYEES GATHERED ON NOVEMBER 1, 1917, FOR THE UNVEILING OF THE COMPANY'S WAR SERVICE FLAG. FIFTY EMPLOYEES LOST THEIR LIVES IN THE WAR.

Fresh Leadership for Changing Times

Prudential was well-represented in World War I. Nearly 1,800 employees served in the armed forces. Furthermore, as author William Carr noted, "The company organized the 'Prudential Home Guard,' a military unit whose purpose was never quite clear. But the fainthearted could take cheer in the thought that if the Kaiser managed to bring his troops up the Passaic River or into Port Newark, Prudential's latter-day Minutemen were prepared to repel the invader."

The end of that war brought wholesale change to America. As the country roared into the 1920s—firmly gripping its gin and tonic—the restrained Victorianism that governed all matters public and private less than a decade before quickly seemed as remote as a cave painting.

The unfortunate circumstances surrounding Forrest Dryden's departure indicated Prudential was also ready for a fresh start, but its change would not be as drastic as the nation's. Prudential, founded by a Yale alumnus, would be led for many years after World War I by a pack of Princetonians. Edward Duffield succeeded Dryden in 1922, and in many ways, he was just what Prudential needed. The elder Dryden had personally recruited Duffield in 1906 to form Prudential's Law Department, and his extensive experience with company tradition made him an ideal figure to take the enterprise forward (and away from not-so-vague accusations of nepotism).

Although Prudential had new leadership for new times, no one could say Duffield embodied the Roaring Twenties. Nothing could be further from the truth. As Carr noted: "It was while Duffield led it that the company came to be known for 'the three P's: Princeton, Presbyterianism, Prudential.' (Some added a fourth: Prissiness.)" For a wealthy and well-established insurance company only recently recovering from public scrutiny and internal adjustments, Duffield's steadiness, practicality and unfaltering trustworthiness were invaluable.

In times of need, Princetonians habitually look to other Princetonians. Duffield ventured no further than the campus on which he was born into a faculty family and to whose board of trustees he was elected in 1920. (He even served dual roles as Prudential's and Princeton's presidents from 1932 to 1933.) Franklin D'Olier, a fellow Tiger trustee, impressed Duffield, and in 1926, D'Olier joined the company as vice president of administration. He quickly became Duffield's most trusted lieutenant and eventually succeeded him as president. Both men would serve Prudential well. Their presidencies spanned 24 years.

Other changes came to Prudential during the 1920s. The 3-cent weekly premium was discontinued in 1922 (although the nickel version remained intact). In that same year, the first mortgage loan branch was opened in Toronto, and a group insurance plan for home office personnel was begun. Otherwise, bucking the impulsiveness of the times, Prudential steered a conservative course and prospered. As always, increased business required increased office space, and the Gibraltar Building was added to the home office complex. Through a system of enclosed bridges, employees could traverse the entire three-building complex without resorting to galoshes.

The Depression

During the Great Depression, Prudential's innate

PRESIDENT EDWARD DUFFIELD (SEATED, CENTER), WITH THE BOARD OF DIRECTORS, WHICH INCLUDED HIS SUCCESSOR FRANKLIN D'OLIER (SEATED, LEFT), ca. 1930.

conservatism—a trait particularly cultivated under Duffield — protected the company from the harsher ravages suffered by other financial institutions. In response to leaner times, salaries were cut in 1932, but remarkably, no one lost a job during the entire Depression, at least not because of economic conditions. Equally remarkable were the $1.5 billion increase in Prudential's life insurance in force, the $471 million it paid out to its policyholders in dividends and the nearly $400 million it made in policy loans from 1930 to 1935.

Although Prudential's financials were exceptional for the time, they didn't mean that the company went about making money while Americans went without jobs. Prudential was heavily committed to mortgage loans during the Depression—both home and farm.

The Depression tested the company's character. Yet, through it all, John Dryden's vision remained central. Prudential was created to protect the workingman, and it did everything it could for working families at a time when it was hardest to do so. Building such relationships confirmed that a benevolent and clear-headed vision could also be good business. Doubtless, many Prudential mortgage holders who survived the Depression with a roof still over their heads

Prudential was created to protect the workingman, and it did everything it could for working families at a time when it was hardest to do so.

didn't forget who was on their side when life's prospects seemed very dim.

The Presidency of Franklin D'Olier

Franklin D'Olier's strengths were organization and efficient production. When Edward Duffield brought D'Olier in as vice president in charge of administration, his mission was to confront Prudential's bloated and somewhat intransigent bureaucracy.

At least one reason for D'Olier's success in streamlining operations at Prudential was his startling habit of roaming the halls and informally dropping in on employees. Such efforts clearly accomplished two things. First, he learned a great deal about the operations of the company. Second, by the end of his presidency, D'Olier probably knew a higher percentage of employees on a first-name basis than any Prudential chief executive since John Dryden. The fact that such impromptu visits kept people on their toes didn't hurt either.

Soon after assuming the presidency following Duffield's death in 1938, D'Olier tackled another big challenge — the still-nagging issue of mutualization. Though in practice Prudential had operated as a mutual company since 1915, almost 600 shares remained outstanding, not

COLONEL FRANKLIN D'OLIER, WITH HIS WIFE AND DAUGHTER, DURING A FAMILY TRIP. COL. D'OLIER BECAME PRESIDENT OF PRUDENTIAL IN 1938.

to mention the complex related lawsuit waged by the heirs of Noah Blanchard. D'Olier, the master problem solver, unleashed a battalion of Prudential heavyweights to resolve these longrunning matters once and for all. After much wrangling behind closed doors as well as in front of magistrates, an agreement was reached with Blanchard's heirs in 1942. With the approval of the state of New Jersey on March 30, 1943, Prudential became, officially and at long last, a mutual insurance company.

By this time, America had plunged into war with Germany and Japan. World War II tested the proficiency and endurance of those working in Prudential's Claims Department. To speed the settlement of claims, the company decided to accept letters or telegrams from the armed forces as proof of death and seek formal documentation after the disbursement of benefits. By June 30, 1946, Prudential had paid more than $70 million on almost 100,000 policies.

According to company records, 6,412 men and women from Prudential served in uniform, and 111 gave their lives. With so many Prudential personnel committed to the war effort, staffing became an issue. One response was to hire and promote women into positions heretofore reserved for men.

The country, like the company, was big and primed for change. Within a few short years, neither America nor Prudential would ever be the same.

Despite being short-staffed, the company contributed to the war effort in many ways. Prudential's printing plant churned out waterproof survival maps for Allied pilots who might be downed in unfamiliar territory. Prudential volunteers donated blood and worked in military canteens and hospitals.

Moreover, D'Olier also assigned two top staff members to accomplish what many thought logistically impossible. Going door to door throughout New Jersey's 21 voting precincts, civilian defense volunteers confirmed the voting status of soldiers, determined their military assignments and mailed proxy forms. Thanks to Prudential, every New Jersey citizen serving in the war could vote in the 1944 election.

D'Olier himself contributed greatly. New York Mayor Fiorello LaGuardia, then also serving as national director of civilian defense, appointed D'Olier the director of all defense issues related to the citizens of New York, New Jersey and Delaware. But D'Olier wouldn't be satisfied until he could hear gunfire. His chance came in 1944 when he accepted the offer to head up the United States Strategic Bombing Survey.

After accepting his military assignment, D'Olier's presence was seldom felt around Prudential. When the war ended, the colonel was in his late 60s. After the strain of travel and the pressure of the war effort, he retired.

In 1926, when D'Olier arrived at Prudential, John Dryden had been dead for 14 years. But through Edward Duffield, the Prudential that Dryden did so much to create was essentially the same Prudential D'Olier inherited when he

(FROM LEFT) DOLORES MONETTI, MARGARET SOUTHARD AND RUTH MOWEN FOLD WATERPROOF SURVIVAL MAPS FOR ALLIED PILOTS IN THE COMPANY'S PRINTING PLANT DURING WORLD WAR II.

became president. By the end of D'Olier's tenure, however, Prudential was a giant company — most surely exceeding Dryden's greatest dreams. On the first day of 1946, Carrol Shanks took over as the seventh president of the company at a time when America had just emerged from a monumental war. The country, like the company, was big and primed for change. For both, it was the end of an era. Within a few short years, neither America nor Prudential would ever be the same.

"He Shook Up the Organization"

Shanks progressed quickly up the ladder. At the age of 47, he was named president of Prudential and became the youngest head of a major life insurance company in North America. He would also engineer one of the most drastic and productive cultural changes in the company's history.

Over the years, Prudential had held to a rigid seniority system. The company's seemingly inexorable prosperity had allowed some dead wood to settle within the organization, some of it floating toward the top. Consequently, doing business according to an inherited Prudential model had been consistently and exclusively rewarded. With Shanks, such habitual thinking would end.

Orville Beal, who would later become president, once said of Shanks: "He didn't hesitate to spend money to modernize the company and its facilities. He made momentous decisions, sometimes against the advice of his top officers, and those acts paid big dividends." Echoing the kind of cultural change that the company would undertake at the end of the century, Shanks prodded people to spend money on research and to explore more original forms of thinking and innovative methods of doing business. "Sometimes, he was too impatient. Sometimes, he was a little too rough on people," Beal said. "But he shook up the organization. He ... got us going again."

Through its first 70 years, Prudential had been lucky in having just the leadership it needed: the visionary Dryden to give it its character, the inspiring and steadfast Duffield when the industry as a whole was being pilloried, the efficient and organized D'Olier at the point when the company was mired in excessive bureaucracy and red tape. And in Carrol Shanks, Prudential had once again found its man.

Not surprisingly, many weren't pleased by the upheaval. But those who remained were a hardy, resilient lot. It would be easy to say they were Shanks' "yes men." But that assumption would be wrong. The folks who remained knew they were valued for brains and creativity, a willingness to take risks and think independently. In retrospect, such were the qualities obviously

CARROL SHANKS, PRESIDENT FROM 1946 TO 1960, BROUGHT TO THE COMPANY A NEW VISION FOR A MODERN PRUDENTIAL. HIS DESIRE FOR EXPANSION REINVIGORATED THE COMPANY AND ITS INVESTORS.

most needed at Prudential at the time. Several of the bunch—Beal, Louis Menagh, Donald MacNaughton, Kenneth Foster—would lead Prudential in the decades to come.

Spread It All Over the Country

The streamlining that Shanks initiated invigorated the company. Employees sensed that their individual contributions mattered. Profits rose, and unnecessary bureaucratic procedures were eliminated.

But Shanks remained unsatisfied. One source of his discomfort was the company's association with Newark. It had always been amicable, but Shanks felt that maintaining the relationship was at times harder than it should be. He concluded that Prudential had become too dependent upon its one location: "All our eggs are in one basket."

A further problem resulted from the sheer enormity of the company. The anonymity resulting from such vast numbers of employees assembled under one roof made systematic career development difficult. Good people too easily went unnoticed and unrewarded. In addition to strategic issues, there were the practical ones. "By the end of 1948," Carr noted, "there were 11,526 employees ... working in a rabbit warren

More employees would be given broader responsibilities, allowing for a stronger career development strategy and reducing the timidity of a huge organization.

of seven buildings in the heart of Newark."

Robert M. Green, vice president and treasurer, had for some time been sitting on a solution, awaiting the right time to approach Shanks. The solution was radical. As Green put it: "You ought to break the whole thing up in pieces and spread it over the United States and Canada."

Green's plan was no small matter. He wasn't talking about branch field offices but regional home offices that would function with the authority, independence and responsibility then limited to Newark. Departmental executives in each regional home office (soon referred to as RHOs) would answer only to the executive vice president of that office, who would essentially serve as that office's CEO. Paperwork would not be duplicated or centralized in Newark. Intrigued, Shanks asked Green to develop a detailed proposal and further demanded that Green and whomever he enlisted to assist him maintain absolute secrecy.

In a six-page memorandum (buttressed by a compendium of background data the size of the Newark phone book), Green outlined the advantages of his plan: Each regional home office could operate with the efficiency and responsiveness of a smaller company. High-profile regional presences would provide a stronger national identity. More employees would be given broader responsibilities, allowing for a stronger career development strategy and reducing the timidity of a huge organization, whose size encouraged specialization over big-picture thinking.

A TWO-TON PIECE OF THE ROCK OF GIBRALTAR, A GIFT FROM THE BRITISH GOVERNMENT, WAS TRANSPORTED TO LOS ANGELES IN JUNE 1948, WHERE IT FORMED THE WESTERN HOME OFFICE CORNERSTONE.

Green's report also acknowledged the trade-off: Because successful decentralization depended upon allowing each regional home office a great deal of independence and flexibility, Newark would have to willingly loosen the reins. Shanks, never one disposed to hand-wringing, read the memo and gave it the green light.

Heading West

The process described above — from Green's proposal to a special executive committee's eventual approval—took the better part of 1946. In February 1947, the plan was given a final and firm blessing, and soon after that, a team arrived in Los Angeles to establish the Western Home Office, or WHO.

During the transition, simply continuing the daily chores of business was a complicated challenge. A WHO work force, set up in Newark prior to the move, began to disentangle what would soon be WHO documents, such as policy forms and loan and dividend records, from the company's central records department.

But the paperwork symbolized a deeper cultural change within the company. Though still in Newark, the members of the WHO group began to function as if they were already in California. Because they would be working as their own autonomous unit, they had to develop procedures and practices brand-new to Prudential. Their work reflected the changes initiated at the company in the late 1990s: Determining what those new procedures and practices would be required an entirely new way of thinking about what Prudential was and how it did business.

On June 1, 1948, the cornerstone was laid on Prudential Square, the company's Western Home Office. Wisely, Prudential ensured that WHO would be seen as the distinctive change in business strategy that it was. Shanks and WHO's vice president, Harry Volk, visited San Francisco, Denver, Portland, Seattle, Spokane and Salt Lake City in 1948 and 1949, speaking at chambers of commerce as well as at luncheons and dinners with local political and business leaders. Everywhere, Shanks' message was the same: Prudential moved to the West to better serve the West. Decision-making would now come from people who lived in the area and knew its problems and issues. Western money would be for Western projects. The company would provide more efficient responses to Western customers.

As noted earlier, Shanks had wanted to shake up Prudential, discourage habit and reward creativity and originality. Establishing the Western Home Office did just that. Reflecting WHO's new independence, Volk began trying things that would have been impossible under Newark's guardianship. For example, he announced that a district agents conference—"with new high standards for qualification"—would be held in Sun Valley. Such extravagance—Sun Valley!—was unheard of in Newark. But Sun Valley was more strategy than extravagance: Show the best agents the good life—a life that could be theirs if they thought big and worked hard. This kind of experimentation and willingness to take risks was just what Shanks had in mind.

SECOND VICE PRESIDENT WILLIAM COHAGEN GREETS STAFF MANAGER ROBERT PERRAULT OF QUEBEC AND HIS FAMILY AT THE CANADIAN HEAD OFFICE IN TORONTO.

Without question, establishing the Western Home Office was expensive and risky. The success of WHO and, indeed, the future of the entire regional home office concept rested on the numbers that came out of Los Angeles at the end of 1949, WHO's first full year of operation. Volk reported a 20-percent increase in sales in that region over the previous year. He further noted that those figures were 12 percent higher than in 1946, the best year in that region. And he was able to assure Newark that its more intangible objectives had also been met, including better service to policyholders, increased efficiency in internal operations and greater numbers of broadly experienced management-level employees.

Continuing Decentralization

As the West Coast numbers rolled in during WHO's first year, it became clear that the experiment was working. Shanks and his staff prepared to establish regional home offices elsewhere.

On December 9, 1949, Shanks announced that Prudential would place a regional office in Toronto. He told the York Club in Toronto three days later: "Enterprise is strengthened by a move such as ours that creates new centers of initiative. We believe moving general management into the region for which it is responsible releases the creative faculties—the drive and imagination—of our managers." Such language—"centers of initiative," "creative faculties," "drive and imagination"—aptly depicts the essence not only of the decentralization strategy but also of the spirit Shanks wished to imbue within the company.

Establishing a Canadian Home Office was also politically wise. Although Prudential had placed field offices in Canada during the first decade of the century, the business atmosphere north of the border had since changed. Canadian nationalism was blossoming and, along with it, an increased sensitivity to what Canadians perceived as intrusions from non-Canadian businesses.

Prudential had always been a good citizen, having in fact invested more in Canada than it had received. But now was the time to reconfirm Prudential's good intentions. Both Shanks and Green, who was appointed to run the office, made it clear to the prime minister as well as to the Canadian business establishment that placing a home office in Toronto meant that capital created in Canada would be invested there.

The results mirrored those of Los Angeles. A year after setting up the Toronto office, Canadian sales doubled. With Toronto confirming that Los Angeles wasn't a fluke, Prudential went full speed ahead, establishing additional regional home offices.

In short order (at least short for such an enormous undertaking), the following offices were opened:

FROM 1947 TO 1955, PRUDENTIAL ESTABLISHED SIX REGIONAL HOME OFFICES. BY 1969, THE COMPANY ADDED THREE MORE RHOs IN NEWARK, BOSTON AND FORT WASHINGTON, PENNSYLVANIA.

- The Southwestern Home Office in 1952 in Houston.
- The Mid-America Home Office in 1955 in Chicago.
- The South Central Home Office in 1955 in Jacksonville, Florida.
- The North Central Home Office in 1955 in Minneapolis.
- The Northeastern Home Office in 1965 in Boston.
- The Eastern Home Office in 1965 in Newark.
- The Central Atlantic Home Office in 1969 in Fort Washington, Pennsylvania.

The new offices were classy buildings. The 18-story Houston structure housed not only the usual accommodations of a Prudential office, including a lounge, library, auditorium and cafeteria, but also sported an outdoor pool lighted for night swimming, as well as a large Peter Hurd mural in the central rotunda.

But starting the construction was often challenging for the location teams. Prudential knew that if landowners learned the company was shopping for a large building site, prices would skyrocket. For example, Shanks chose a magnificent location for the Chicago office at the north end of Grant Park facing Lake Michigan. The *Chicago Tribune* called it "probably one of the world's most valuable pieces of undeveloped city property." To avoid price gouging, an agent representing "an anonymous party" spent 18

Prudential moved to the West to better serve the West. Decision-making would now come from people who lived in the area and knew its problems and issues.

months negotiating on Prudential's behalf. The extraordinary length of the talks resulted from the fact that Prudential wasn't primarily buying land, but the air rights above railroad tracks of the Illinois Central and Michigan Central rail lines as well as the adjoining Illinois Central station at Randolph Street. None of these structures could be removed, and thus the plot had to be negotiated according to three dimensions.

As with Los Angeles, Prudential's Chicago office prompted an explosion of growth and development around it. Dedicated in 1955, it was the first skyscraper to be built in Chicago in 17 years.

In each city, Prudential carefully represented itself as a good neighbor and was invariably welcomed as such. This approach was clearly a "win-win" for both sides. For example, when the Jacksonville office opened in 1955, it was praised for its benefits to the community and its open house drew tens of thousands of people. In 1958, the *Jacksonville Journal* reported: "[During the previous year alone,] 107 meetings of local civic groups were held in the Prudential auditorium, with more than 28,000 people in attendance. Company employees are in service clubs, on the boards of charitable institutions, on volunteer fire departments, in the leadership of Boy Scout troops and Little League baseball, and involved in many other worthwhile activities. Prudential has become a part of all phases of community life in the Jacksonville area."

And while Prudential leaders took great pride in such announcements, they must also have taken satisfaction in noting that within five

(FROM LEFT) PRUDENTIAL VICE PRESIDENT JIM RUTHERFORD, CHICAGO MAYOR MARTIN KENNELLY AND AMERICAN BRIDGE PRESIDENT NORMAN OBBARD AT THE MID-AMERICA HOME OFFICE DEDICATION IN 1955.

years of SCHO's opening, sales in the ten-state region had tripled.

Union Discontent

In 1950, Prudential was 75 years old. The company observed the anniversary on February 28th with a Founder's Day luncheon honoring the birthday of its first president, Allen Bassett. For one afternoon, a massive enterprise took a moment to recall its beginnings in a basement office in Newark. Among the 225 guests were 22 descendents of Prudential's first four presidents: Bassett, Blanchard, Dryden and Duffield. On this occasion, one could easily reflect upon how much had changed and how quickly Prudential had grown. Carrol Shanks and company were courageously leading a prosperous and respected company, one in the midst of spreading its name and products even farther afield.

Under Shanks—indeed, under all its presidents—Prudential had never been a company to gloat. As shown by its ambitious decentralization, Prudential always felt there were opportunities to make things better for itself and for present and future customers.

Prudential was ready and eager for a new challenge, and it would soon get one, from a most unexpected and frankly unwelcome place: within. Its agents were about to stage a massive strike. If the company were ever tempted to gloat, this matter would stop it cold.

In 1951, district agents walked out for 81 days—the largest and longest white-collar labor dispute in the nation's history at that time. A portion of Prudential's agents had been organized as early as 1942, and relations generally had been amicable. But by the early '50s, tensions had been increasing between Prudential and the American Federation of Labor, which represented the agents. In Pittsburgh, Prudential had to suspend several agents in January 1951. In protest, 2,300 agents called in sick. A week after the suspensions, 1,600 agents demonstrated unannounced in front of the home office in Newark.

AGENTS PICKET OUTSIDE A NEW YORK CITY DISTRICT OFFICE IN 1951. THE STRIKE, THE FIRST AND ONLY IN THE COMPANY'S HISTORY, ENDED IN FEBRUARY 1952.

Relationships failed to improve. As a union contract was being unsuccessfully negotiated during the winter of 1951, the AFL called a strike, which would last from December 1st of that year until February 20, 1952. It was the first and only strike in Prudential's history.

Both sides suffered. Agents and their families were forced to do without pay through the holiday season. Prudential, ill-equipped to deal with labor strife, kept hoping the matter could be settled quickly. In the end, both sides were probably surprised at the event's duration and stridency.

The Prudential leadership was reviled, often publicly. Orville Beal, then executive vice president in charge of district agents, took it particularly hard. Beal, mild-mannered and personable, himself the son of an agent, had always felt a particular affinity with those in the field. Even after being promoted to vice president, he was often known to accompany agents on their rounds, an activity he felt helped him stay in touch with the all-important face-to-face aspect of the business. But at the time of the strike, his sole contact with the field consisted of entering the home office to the accompaniment of sneers and insults.

Beal might have felt better had he walked the gauntlet alongside Shanks—for whom the strikers saved their most venomous epithets. But Shanks was tough, and those who knew him also knew that he had never paid much attention to popularity polls. To him, respectability and steadfastness ranked much higher as measures of character. To make this point during the strike, Shanks often had his driver drop him off blocks from the home office's main entrance. From there, he would proceed through the throng of angry agents—bolt upright, head held high—and take his licks without blinking.

But Shanks' unflinching demeanor should not be mistaken for a lack of caring—about either the company or its employees. When the strike finally ended, it was clear he had learned a great deal and saw in the occasion another opportunity to shake the company out of the bureaucratic complacency and institutional

Prudential was ready and eager for a new challenge, and it would soon get one, from a most unexpected and frankly unwelcome place: within.

inertia he'd been fighting throughout his presidency.

In his history, Carr cited a small example of how Shanks responded: "Not long after the strike, Shanks told some of his men in top management that he wanted the company's field offices all over the country modernized, including the introduction of air conditioning. A few days later he was presented with a plan for air-conditioning every Prudential office in the U.S. and Canada over a period of three years. 'Three years!' he exclaimed. 'I want it done in three weeks.' And in a matter of weeks it was done."

TWO EMPLOYEES INSPECT AN ELECTRONIC CALCULATING MACHINE IN 1954. A YEAR LATER, PRUDENTIAL PURCHASED FROM IBM THE "650" AND "702" MODELS FOR USE IN ITS OFFICES NATIONWIDE.

The First Computers

If one asked John Dryden what life insurance was all about, he'd surely have asserted, without a pause, that it was about providing security for working-class families. But if at any time in Prudential's history, you directed the same question to someone in the operations side of the business, the answer would have been "numbers." Getting them right. Tracking them. Updating. Adjusting. We now call it "data processing."

In the earliest years of the industry, hands processed the data, and few found it a pleasure. While statistical accuracy was and remains supremely important, office technology was most certainly invented to free the human mind for more creative endeavors. For this reason, Prudential took an active lead in data processing from the beginning. In tracing the development of mechanical and electronic computing, historians date the start of Prudential's contributions to the

field as far back as the 19th century. John K. Gore, then the company's actuary, drew up plans for a perforating machine and card sorter. His brother-in-law, a mechanical engineer, created the machines based on Gore's concept. Installed in 1895, they were used well into the 1930s.

In the 1940s, Harvard University began extensive experiments designed to develop digital computers, and Prudential gladly volunteered to test their applicability. In 1947, Henry Schrimpf Jr. of Prudential's Methods Division reported, "We have been discussing for some months a certain type of electronic sequence-controlled calculator for premium billing and other insurance company work. Our experience in this trial convinces us that such a calculator will work."

As expected, developing such a complex device took years. In 1955, International Business Machines delivered two models, one to the home office and another to Toronto. By 1967, Prudential had 52 computers running around the clock.

A Grand Dame Takes a Powder

Carrol Shanks literally changed the face of Prudential with his 1955 decision to demolish the Prudential Building, John Dryden's grand Victorian dame and monument to stability and opulence. She presided over the heart of Newark for more than 60 years, and many regretted the departure of such a bustled and brocaded testament to another era. The company's new quarters—the 26-story, white-marble Plaza Building—was as unadorned as Dryden's had been elaborate. Yet few would deny that

Prudential Plaza more appropriately reflected the leaner, modernized Prudential.

One mark of this new post-war Prudential — a major one, in fact — was in the development of new products. The first flourish came from, of all places, group insurance. Prudential had always dabbled in group — in 1898, it wrote a policy covering the married couples employed by Montgomery Ward in Chicago — but for reasons both of personnel and organizational structure, group had never received the company's sustained attention.

Like many other areas under Shanks' purview, this oversight would change. Edmund Whittaker, a gifted, rambunctious Scotsman, was charged with giving the Group Department the focus and development it needed. He was blessed with creativity, charisma and boundless energy. There was no better man for the job. By 1949, after little more than five years under Whittaker's leadership, group operations were setting records. "For the first time in the history of the Prudential," wrote Whittaker in his annual departmental report, "our Group life insurance production exceeded that of any other company, and by a very large margin. Our 1949 Group life volume of $589 million is not only the largest ever written by the Prudential, but is the largest ever produced in one year by an insurance company."

A NEW PRUDENTIAL EMERGED IN THE 1950s THROUGH CHANGE AND GROWTH, MARKED BY CONSTRUCTION OF THE PLAZA BUILDING AND THE DEMOLITION OF THE HOME OFFICE'S VICTORIAN-ERA BUILDINGS.

The transition of group insurance from undervalued to profitable resource aptly illustrates a basic Prudential characteristic. In its first century in particular, Prudential rarely innovated, but no company was better at taking a good idea and refining it to produce an extraordinary product. This attribute was true with the company's work in the complex area of pension benefits during the post-World War II era. One example was PRISA, the company's Property Investment Separate Account, which was established to give pension planners an opportunity to put a portion of their funds into real estate to diversify their investments in stocks and bonds.

In a similar move toward the diversification of pension funds, Prudential rolled out its Flexible Funding Facility in 1966 for clients who wanted not only freedom as to the timing and movement of their contributions, but also flexibility in the use of Prudential's annuities. Between 1950 and 1975, the Group Pension Division, like the rest of group, expanded enormously, accounting for more than 27 percent of Prudential's assets by 1974.

The Agent Gets Respect

Regardless of the fundamental merit of the product, persuading someone to buy insurance has never been easy. Modern buyers are now more

In its first century Prudential rarely innovated, but no company was better at taking a good idea and refining it to produce an extraordinary product.

sophisticated, particularly regarding comprehensive and long-range financial matters, and during much of Prudential's first 75 years, Americans viewed insurance salesmen as today's consumers look upon telemarketers. Back then, selling a policy required an element of intrusiveness, followed by some crafty play upon the potential buyer's conscience.

In the early years of the company, it was difficult to develop and enforce professional standards among agents because the work was so harsh. Six days a week of face-to-face selling was often depressing and full of rejection and self-doubt. Every insurance company struggled to retain the few good sales agents willing to endure such conditions. And many weren't very good. As one Prudential vice president said in 1975: "A half-century ago, few of our agents were really salesmen who knew their products. Most of them were simply premium collectors. It used to be said that streetcar conductors made the best recruits because they made change real good."

In the seminal works on life insurance, selling is rarely mentioned. Prudential possessed the same blind spot. Until mid-century, Prudential paid little attention to the sales agent —whether it was in recruitment and training, self-

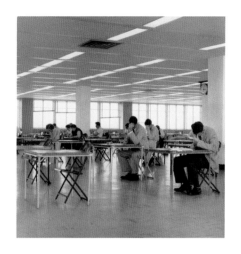

IN THE 1950s, PRUDENTIAL ESTABLISHED A NEW TESTING SYSTEM TO HELP IDENTIFY TOP CANDIDATES, GREATLY IMPROVING THE TRAINING PROCESS FOR NEW RECRUITS.

image, character or career development.

Like many other aspects of life at Prudential after World War II, those circumstances were about to change. Harold Stewart, Shanks' executive vice president for field operations, wasn't the most popular man at the company, but perhaps because his father had been an agent, he had real empathy for the challenges of selling insurance. Under Stewart, tests were administered to identify top candidates, and training became more organized. Stewart's most significant acknowledgment of the importance of agency work came in a new requirement for personnel within the District Agencies Department: They could not expect executive positions unless they had field experience.

Over the next three decades, Prudential's practices regarding agents were refined, and the attention paid off. By 1973, the percentage of new ordinary life business sold through district agencies more than doubled from the previous decade.

Other initiatives contributed to the increase. Capitalizing in the 1960s on the growing presence of computers throughout Prudential, the company introduced the Business Valuation and Estate Conservation programs, both of which offered the customer computer-generated personalized insurance plans. Computers were also enlisted in

Six days a week of face-to-face selling was full of rejection. Every company struggled to retain the good sales agents willing to endure such conditions.

support of the venerable Dollar Guide, first introduced in 1947 and still in use three decades later. In 1956, Prudential began offering its family policy, which not only covered the life of a husband and wife, but also automatically included each child as he or she was born. The family policy immediately became Prudential's most popular coverage. In the policy's first four months on the market, a quarter-million families signed up for $1.5 billion worth of new insurance.

As a result of better recruiting and training as well as more sophisticated sales instruments and products, the sales agent, no longer the neglected foot soldier of the company, gradually attained a well-deserved professional status.

Increased Investments

Until the 1950s, Prudential's investment strategies resembled the insurance industry's in general. They were conservative: blue chips all the way. Not surprisingly—and against the advice of those directly in charge of Prudential's investments at that time—Shanks wished to expand and diversify. To that end, Shanks established the commercial and industrial Loan Department in 1956 to handle small- and medium-sized transactions. It was the right time for such a move. The recently established regional home offices made Prudential next-door neighbors to a large number of individuals and institutions in need of capital. In the decade since the war, Prudential had done very well. *Time* magazine soon reported the results: "In every U.S. activity there is Pru

AIDED BY SALES TOOLS LIKE THE DOLLAR GUIDE, AGENTS WERE ABLE TO COMMUNICATE MORE EFFICIENTLY WITH CUSTOMERS, INCREASING SALES GREATLY THROUGH THE 1950s AND 1960s.

money, from cattle and cotton to guided-missile factories, race tracks, and country clubs."

This diversification strategy soon spread to the company's Real Estate Investment Department. Because increased competition had lowered the profit potential for residential mortgages, Prudential began to focus on commercial and industrial mortgages and long-term real estate ownership. Its holdings and investments soon included 55 Water Street in Manhattan (weighing in at 3.25 million square feet, the largest privately owned office building in the United States) as well as the Empire State Building and Chicago's Merchandise Mart. Prudential's real estate strategy wasn't the clumsy, "buy-in-bulk" practice found in similar-sized companies. Each investment either sprang from or was under the scrutiny of one of Prudential's 58 mortgage loan offices.

To offset potential inflationary pressures in other investment areas, Prudential also began in 1950 to invest in common stocks. By the mid-'70s, the company's common stock portfolios were valued at more than $4 billion, the largest in the life insurance industry.

The Resignation of Carrol Shanks

Carrol Shanks had proven himself to be an extraordinary leader in his 15 years as Prudential's president. He was perhaps the first true visionary and creative thinker in that role since John Dryden himself. Only a man so willing to "think outside the box" could have refashioned such an enormous, cumbersome operation in such positive and radical ways, enabling and rewarding creativity and initiative and enlivening Prudential in both body and spirit. Few could have predicted that he would leave the company under a cloud of scrutiny.

It began simply enough with a substantial personal investment in some Western timberland from which Shanks stood to profit considerably. However, the transaction involved Georgia-Pacific, whose chairman sat on Prudential's board while Shanks sat on Georgia-Pacific's. In early 1960, *The Wall Street Journal* picked up on this connection and ran with it, suggesting an insider deal. Shanks eagerly disclosed all details of the investment and contended there was no wrongdoing. The New Jersey commissioner of banking and insurance investigated and found nothing illegal, but Shanks, wishing to avoid further bad publicity for himself and Prudential, quickly rid himself of the property.

The sale wasn't enough. Skittish, Prudential appointed its own committee to investigate. What all investigating parties concluded had already been put forth in a rebuttal by Shanks himself: An unwritten and uncodified understanding exists that executives of mutual insurance companies do not enjoy the same freedom to invest as executives in other businesses. Again, as Shanks emphasized, no legal issue was involved, merely

PRESIDENT LOUIS MENAGH (RIGHT), WITH REAL ESTATE MAGNATE LAWRENCE WIEN (LEFT), DURING A 1961 PRESS CONFERENCE ANNOUNCING THE COMPANY'S PURCHASE OF THE EMPIRE STATE BUILDING.

an unpremeditated breach of protocol. Nonetheless, at the request of the company, Shanks resigned in December 1960.

For two years after the resignation, New Jersey and, to some degree, New York continued to investigate the matter and, for all their efforts, found nothing illegal.

A Tightening of the Reins

Shanks was replaced by 68-year-old Louis Menagh. While Prudential had done very well under its willful and radical postwar president, it was time for a corrective. The company's soaring profits in the mid-'50s had prompted Shanks to overexpand, and it was now up to the more conservative Menagh to reduce the resulting administrative expenses.

Menagh was already near retirement age, and it was probably understood that his tenure wouldn't last long. In fact, one of the major tasks before him was to do what Shanks hadn't: groom a successor. Within a year of assuming the presidency, the board announced that Orville Beal would be promoted to senior executive vice president, a new title within the company and a clear sign that Beal would soon take over the top job.

He indeed became president soon thereafter

Over time, Beal reduced the average age of the board of directors from 72 to 58 and accomplished much the same within the senior executive ranks.

—on October 1, 1962. Beal followed Menagh in correcting imbalances that had arisen during Shanks' presidency. Over time, Beal reduced the average age of the board of directors from 72 to 58 and accomplished much the same within the senior executive ranks.

But a more difficult task awaited him. Beal had been with Prudential since Edward Duffield's presidency and was now in his fourth decade of company service. As an able lieutenant throughout Shanks' administration, Beal had witnessed that leader's many improvements, but he had also noted the negative side effects. Whatever Shanks' intentions, he had created a cult of personality or, to be more accurate, personalities. Not only did the headstrong Shanks create a "for me or against me" mentality, he had also fostered a climate in which executives became identified with their sponsors.

In some cases, as with the extraordinary Charles Campbell, employees benefited because Campbell was a great mentor, training future leaders and then pushing them forward. But Beal was aware that other spheres of influence had become fiefdoms. While the pre-Shanks Prudential was perhaps a little somnolent and less nimble, it had always thought of itself as one company with a single mission. In the post-Shanks Prudential, what had once been functional departments were now enclaves. Executives competed rather than communicated, producing a certain amount of rancor.

Beal needed to reunify the company. To that purpose, the Special Committee on Home Office Organization was formed in May 1963. Under the chairmanship of Donald MacNaughton (who

ORVILLE BEAL, WHO BEGAN HIS CAREER WITH THE COMPANY AS AN AUDIT CLERK IN 1926, TOOK THE REINS AS PRUDENTIAL'S NINTH PRESIDENT ON OCTOBER 1, 1962.

would later become president himself), the committee was to examine and make recommendations regarding the structure of the entire company.

The committee first undertook what it thought would be the simple task of reviewing the company's history over the past quarter-century. Much to its chagrin, it discovered that, for all the monumental changes since the war, little information had been documented and preserved. The committee then set out to interview hundreds of executives and other personnel and dissect the seminal events of the past decade to characterize and define the basic presumptions behind Prudential's decision-making.

From the recommendations of the committee's study, the company began a full-scale reorganization in 1965. The first element was the establishment of an Eastern Home Office (EHO), which covered New York City, Long Island and New Jersey as well as Pennsylvania, Delaware, Maryland and the District of Columbia. This division of territory would last only three years. By 1968, EHO had become too cumbersome. As a result, the Central Atlantic Home Office was built in Fort Washington, Pennsylvania, to assume responsibility for all but New York and New Jersey.

Establishing the EHO freed the corporate home office from daily production responsibilities, allowing it to concentrate on planning, policy-making, coordination, evaluation and control. The special committee recommended that the corporate home office be restructured into four areas reflecting responsibilities—corporate services, insurance, investments, and planning and control—and suggested that an executive vice president head each of the four divisions.

In 1965, the company also built new quarters for the Northeastern Home Office in Boston. The $150 million Prudential Center opened with great fanfare and, like other Prudential regional offices, helped jump-start Boston's sagging city center by turning, as Beal put it, "an old blighted freight yard ... into the largest unified civic, business and residential complex in the world."

VICE PRESIDENT THOMAS ALLSOPP (RIGHT) LOOKS ON AS BOSTON MAYOR JOHN F. COLLINS ADDS HIS SIGNATURE TO THE BEAM USED TO TOP OFF THE PRUDENTIAL CENTER'S CONSTRUCTION IN 1964.

Responding to Societal Unrest

The last half of the 1960s was dominated by an unpopular war in Southeast Asia and societal unrest at home. Headquartered in Newark, Prudential was strongly affected by the latter. On July 13, 1967, the city was torn apart by riots. Similar disturbances followed in Los Angeles and other cities. That same year, Beal and MacNaughton responded with an assessment of the company's role as a corporate citizen, both in the city of Newark and around the country.

One of the basic premises behind Prudential's founding was the belief that institutions, even those obligated to make a profit, have a responsibility to improve society. Beal and MacNaughton determined it was time to re-examine the company in light of that mission and make certain that Prudential was fully sensitive to the new needs arising from this critical period in America's history.

As a preliminary step, the company publicly reasserted its commitment to equal employment opportunity for everyone, regardless of race, sex, color or national origin. Beal didn't stop there. As president of the Institute of Life Insurance, he announced the industry would commit $2 billion in investment aid to the riot-torn cities. By 1972, Prudential alone had earmarked more than $333 million for the program. When Kenneth Gibson was elected Newark's first African-American mayor in 1970, he requested and received long-term assistance from Prudential, which deployed a vice president to serve almost exclusively as Newark's business administrator. Mayor Tom Bradley of Los Angeles, when elected in 1974, made a similar request, and again Prudential responded.

Internally, the company became more aggressive in its recruitment of women and minorities, and in 1974, it created a Public Affairs Department, in part to ensure that community service programs remained an ongoing aspect of the company's operation. In announcing the new department, MacNaughton stated, "We have been convinced for a long time now that it is of paramount importance

MacNaughton charged his leaders to think more creatively and to develop and reward those below them for their talents as unconventional thinkers.

for Prudential to strengthen its role in American society by making the conduct of our business as responsive as possible to the needs of our policyholders, our employees and society as a whole."

"The Rock at the Top"

The '60s challenged Prudential to improve its role as a corporate citizen, but it was also a decade in which the company's business affairs continued to flourish. In 1966, the company moved ahead of the Met and into first place in assets. In an article entitled "The Rock at the Top," *Fortune* magazine wrote, "Prudential is treating its new distinction with modesty. In its press release summarizing 1966's results, the company took no note at all of its asset position relative to the rest of the insurance industry, saying simply that 'the Prudential Insurance Company recorded 1966 as one of its finest years.' Actually, it was also one of Metropolitan's finest years."

The MacNaughton Presidency

Perhaps no top executive had been better prepared to take over a company than Donald MacNaughton in 1969 when Orville Beal retired. Having chaired the Special Committee on Home Office Organization, MacNaughton possessed a comprehensive understanding of company operations. In his first speech as president to the Prudential President's Council, MacNaughton reiterated that while Prudential must maintain a firm sense of public duty, its business was selling insurance. "The company was created to sell, and today, nearly 100 years later, that is still our primary function—to sell,"

DONALD MACNAUGHTON ARRIVES FOR A VISIT TO THE NORTHEASTERN HOME OFFICE IN BOSTON. MACNAUGHTON'S PRESIDENCY WAS MARKED WITH A RENEWED SENSE OF CORPORATE CITIZENSHIP.

he said. "Too often, we get so involved in the complexities of the enterprise or in our own particular responsibility that we lose sight of what we are really trying to do—which is to sell."

By placing such an emphasis on selling, MacNaughton was doing more than just trying to increase the bottom line. Like Art Ryan at the end of the century, MacNaughton was pushing the company to think more comprehensively. Continued prosperity required a focus beyond the limitations of the company's specific business functions and toward the needs of the customer.

MacNaughton knew that customers had more financial needs than just life insurance and Prudential must change to take advantage of these opportunities. MacNaughton's address outlined his intentions to move the company into areas outside Prudential's traditional spheres of operation: "We will also expand in areas that are not directly customer-oriented in the traditional life insurance sense. ... I think our minds should not be closed to the possibility of any service which may be related to our traditional lines of business." MacNaughton charged his leaders to think more creatively and to develop and reward those below them for their talents as unconventional thinkers.

In 1970, MacNaughton was appointed to a new post to accommodate a necessary reorganization. He became Prudential's chairman of the board and chief executive officer. Kenneth Foster succeeded MacNaughton as president, and Robert Beck filled Foster's place as executive vice president in charge of marketing.

Other changes followed. December 1973

saw the introduction of the Advanced Ordinary System (AOS), which the company described as "one of the five largest and most complex computer application systems ever developed, ... comparable in size and scope to the government's SAC [Strategic Air Command] and space programs." AOS had been in development for 10 years, handled 11 million policies and processed 550,000 transactions each night, an astounding number at that time.

Not only was the system more powerful than any previously developed for the industry, it was also the most flexible. Prudential's first wave of computers, though all created by IBM, were of varying models. Installed in the Newark home office and high-density regional home offices, they were unable to communicate with one another. AOS solved this problem and did more. New data could be added faster and in greater quantity, and the entire system could be periodically updated. It soon became standard procedure to insert about 2,000 system changes every three months, essentially providing the company with a new computer system on a quarterly basis.

In 1973, Foster retired as president and was replaced by Beck, the first man since John Dryden to rise from agent to president. Beck, who first sold insurance while a paratrooper in World War II, was also remarkable for his youth. At 47, he was one of the youngest men to hold the second-in-command position in a company of Prudential's size.

With Beck, Prudential continued its good

PRUDENTIAL'S SALES HIT A RECORD $17.6 BILLION IN 1970, THE SAME YEAR THAT KENNETH FOSTER (RIGHT) SUCCEEDED DONALD MACNAUGHTON AS COMPANY PRESIDENT.

fortune of having the right kind of leadership at the right time. To carry out MacNaughton's plans for diversification, the company needed Beck's experience as a former head of Prudential's marketing department. But even more, it needed his strength as a planner. Throughout the decade, Bob Beck's leadership and his influence on the future of the company would prove invaluable.

Continuing to Change While Keeping Its Focus

As Prudential's first century drew to a close, the company stepped further into diverse new products and services. By the end of 1974, PRUPAC, or the Prudential Property and Casualty Insurance Company, was operating in almost every state. The PIC Realty Corporation was formed to develop and manage real estate. The Prudential Reinsurance Company put the company into the reinsurance field. In an even bolder departure, PruLease, Prudential's first acquisition in 1974, specialized in leasing nuclear fuel cores, vehicles, and other equipment to utilities, industrial companies and banks.

In 1971, the Pruco Securities Corporation was founded to broker securities for the investment portfolios Prudential managed. GIB Laboratories marketed chemical analyses and other life insurance-related laboratory services. Two Canadian subsidiaries were opened to handle real estate investment and the management of a Prudential-developed mutual fund.

Throughout this flurry of creativity, the bottom line increased admirably. Between 1968 and 1975, sales almost tripled from $13.9 billion of life insurance to almost $31 billion. Life insurance in force increased from $137 billion to more than $236 billion, and assets rose from $26.6 billion to almost $40 billion. A year prior to its centennial, Prudential outperformed the Met by every financial gauge that measures which is the largest insurance company in the United States.

In times of such rapid and far-reaching diversification, other companies have stumbled on the most obvious rock in the road: They've forgotten who they are. In a remarkable commendation to Prudential's character (and MacNaughton's comprehensive vision), the company managed to keep its primary focus on

CHAIRMAN ROBERT A. BECK (FAR RIGHT) MEETS WITH SCHOOL REPRESENTATIVES TO DISCUSS PLANS FOR THE $1 MILLION CORPORATE FUND DRIVE FOR NEW JERSEY'S INDEPENDENT COLLEGES IN 1979.

those it served first—its policyholders.

That steadfastness of vision would have possibly been the only thing recognizable to John Dryden had he walked through the doors of the Newark home office a century after he had founded The Prudential Insurance Company of America. Perhaps, initially, the strangeness would upset him. But it's not stretching things to imagine the following scenario: Don MacNaughton takes his arm at the door, hands him a centennial policy and explains all it can do for a policyowner, displays the galaxy of regional home offices and the contributions they've made to their communities, and perhaps does a trick or two at the computer bank. Once he recovered his balance, Mr. Dryden would walk out a proud man indeed.

A year prior to its centennial, Prudential outperformed the Met by every financial gauge that measures which is the largest insurance company in the United States.

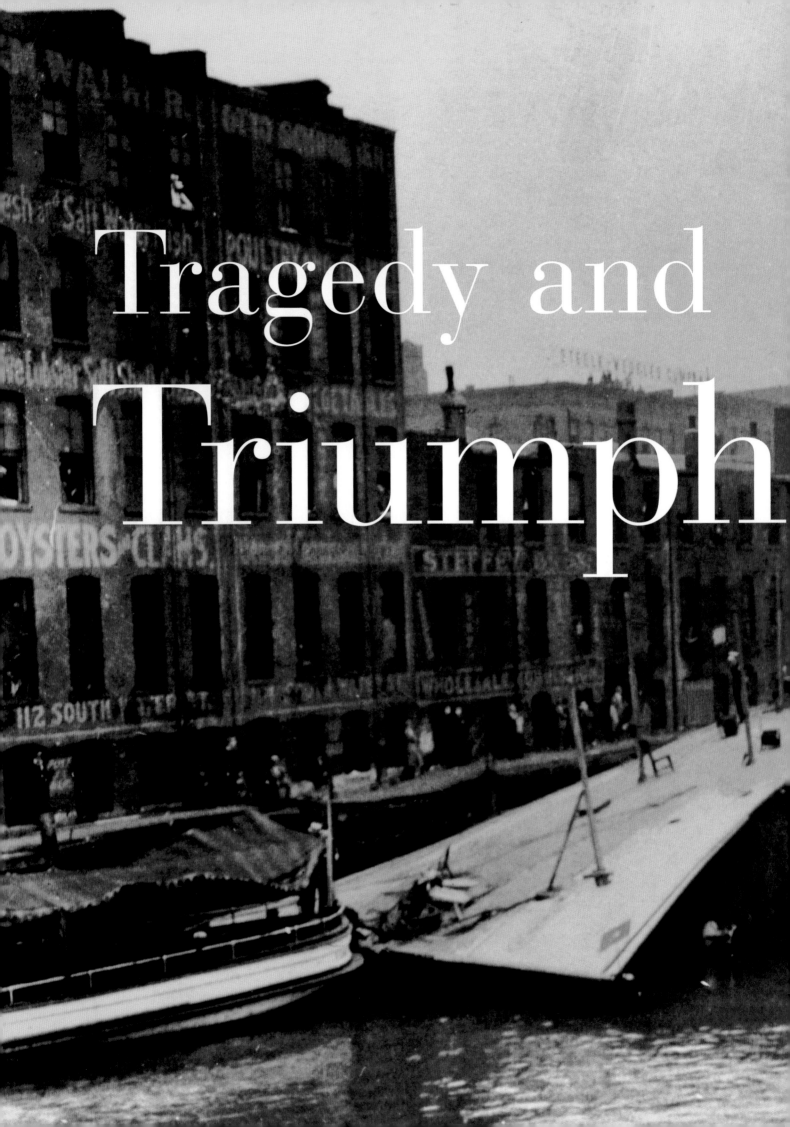

Tragedy and Triumph

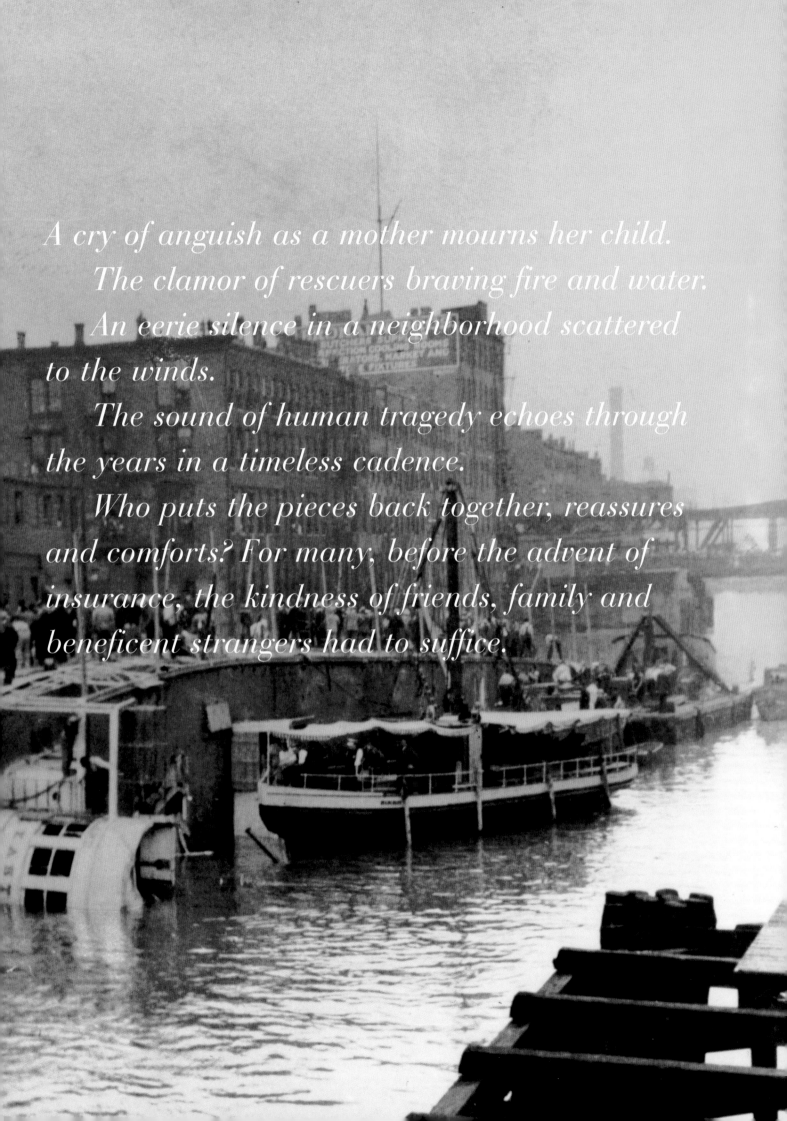

A cry of anguish as a mother mourns her child.

The clamor of rescuers braving fire and water.

An eerie silence in a neighborhood scattered to the winds.

The sound of human tragedy echoes through the years in a timeless cadence.

Who puts the pieces back together, reassures and comforts? For many, before the advent of insurance, the kindness of friends, family and beneficent strangers had to suffice.

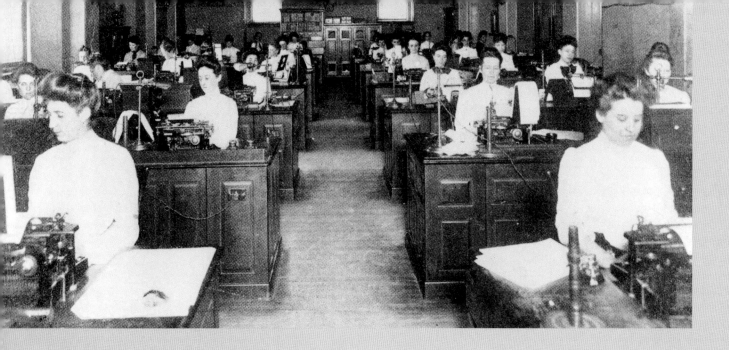

Since the development in the mid-19th century of the modern system of casualty, property and life insurance, the responsibility for "making people whole" has shifted in large part to companies such as Prudential.

Although the comfort these companies have brought to families has gone unchanged, the risks against which their insurance is written have not. The Great Fire of London in 1666, for example, spurred the growth of fire insurance, and well into the 19th century, the danger of fire was one of the most fearsome risks of life.

As the 20th century brought new worries,

PRECEDING PAGE: THE *EASTLAND* CAPSIZED IN THE CHICAGO RIVER, JULY 24, 1915, CLAIMING THE LIVES OF 224 INDUSTRIAL POLICYHOLDERS AMONG 800 VICTIMS. *ABOVE:* INDUSTRIAL DIVISION STENOGRAPHERS IN THE HOME OFFICE, ca. 1915. *OPPOSITE (TOP):* TWENTY-ONE INDUSTRIAL POLICYHOLDERS DIED FROM AN ATTACK ON THE BATTLESHIP *MAINE,* FEBRUARY 15, 1898, IN HAVANA HARBOR, CUBA. *OPPOSITE (BOTTOM):* CLAIM DEPARTMENT, ca. 1901.

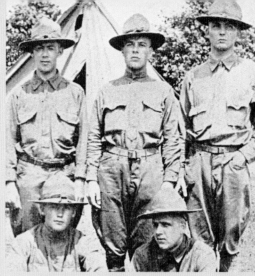

modern insurance coverage expanded to assuage them. Advances in transportation technology, the growth of urban areas and Americans' ever-increasing longevity brought new risks—and new challenges.

Tragedy on a large scale became familiar to us in the 20th century as disasters such as the influenza epidemic of 1918, the Dust Bowl of the 1930s and the 1992 devastation from

OPPOSITE: PRUDENTIAL RED CROSS UNIT, 1918. *ABOVE (CLOCKWISE):* A MEMBER OF THE SERVICEMEN'S MUSICAL REVUE PERFORMING FOR INJURED SOLDIERS, ca. 1944; PRUDENTIAL EMPLOYEES SERVING IN THE ARMY AT CAMP EDGE, SEA GIRT, NEW JERSEY, 1917; IN 1991, THE PRUDENTIAL FOUNDATION DONATED MONEY TO ADD NAMES TO AND MAINTAIN THE VIETNAM VETERANS MEMORIAL.

Prudential Loan
186046.

A TRACTOR LIES BURIED IN SOIL ON A PRUDENTIAL LOAN-BACKED, SOUTH DAKOTA FARM, 1935. *BELOW:* THE REAL ESTATE AND LOAN DEPARTMENT, ca. 1930.

PRUDENTIAL HALL

Hurricane Andrew took their toll on millions. The very nature of Prudential's mission places its people at the scene of human suffering all too often. But that mission also enables its people to serve the most basic of human needs and to ensure that out of the midst of tragedy— any tragedy—the human spirit rises in triumph.

OPPOSITE (CLOCKWISE): CEO ARTHUR RYAN (SECOND FROM RIGHT) VISITS THE NEW JERSEY PERFORMING ARTS CENTER IN NEWARK DURING CONSTRUCTION, 1996; CLAIMS ADJUSTERS MEET WITH A HOME OWNER TO ASSESS DAMAGE CAUSED BY HURRICANE ANDREW, 1992; CONSTRUCTION SITE OF THE PLAZA BUILDING IN NEWARK, VIEWED FROM BROAD STREET, ca. 1960; THE PRUDENTIAL-SPONSORED, GATEWAY IV BUSINESS COMPLEX, NEWARK, 1988. *ABOVE:* HOMES LEVELED BY HURRICANE ANDREW.

Toward a New Century

Stories of Prudential and Its People

Art Ryan [chairman and CEO] has talked about getting rid of "The" in The Prudential Insurance Company of America, and it reminds me of a story when I was an attorney for Prudential in Chicago. One day, we received a summons ordering us to appear in U.S. District Court because a gentleman was claiming he owned the "The" in Prudential's name. Yours truly was charged with getting that complaint dismissed.

Opposite: The Prudential Friendly Society officially changed its name to The Prudential Insurance Company of America in 1877. Since then, Prudential has become one of the world's most recognizable names in business.

I went to court and filed papers to dismiss the complaint. The judge was very harried. He said, "Well, we'll set it for briefing." I said, "'Your Honor, please read this thing because setting it for briefing means a lot more work for us and a lot more time."

So, the judge took a couple minutes to look at the complaint. He said, "We'll take it under advisement." About three months later, he dismissed the case. So, Art might become the first one to do it, but he's not the first one to try.

George Coleman, Newark, New Jersey

"We're Constant. And Changing." In the past decade, there's been much talk—almost always with an air of nostalgia—about how much Prudential "has changed." Undoubtedly, the company's outward appearance has been irrevocably transformed over the past quarter-century. Few companies—except manufacturers of buggy whips and mustache wax—have retained their original look. But there's a great difference between a company's external appearance and its internal reality. While some of Prudential's recent changes are indeed profound, they've not altered its essential character.

A decade ago, then-CEO Robert Winters said proudly, "We're Constant. And Changing." Underlying Winters' comment is the simple understanding that no successful company can exist in a vacuum. To thrive, companies must respond to a changing world. Over the past 25 years, the world has changed in three areas of

particular import for Prudential. It has experienced a seismic shift in consumer taste and habits, seen the emergence of a global economy and witnessed a radical transformation of the financial services industry. Another powerful force is at work in each of these areas: rapidly advancing technology. The company's responses to this confluence of forces have been by necessity comprehensive and wide-ranging, but they have hardly altered the character of Prudential.

To begin with, Prudential has listened to its customers and responded to their needs throughout its history, and what they're saying today is something considerably different from 25 years ago. Back then, substantial life insurance was a mainstay of most mainstream households. Today, consumers are as likely to buttress themselves against ill fortune with investments and annuities—saving for a comfortable retirement as well as planning for death.

Prudential has undergone further transformations because of societal changes and technological advances, which have altered consumer habits. A generation ago, a family would purchase its insurance during a visit from an agent—someone they had known perhaps for years. At the close of the century, with both husband and wife in the workplace, families have less time for such personal encounters. Technology has stepped in to solve the problem—

first through enhanced telephone service, then widespread computerization and more recently the omnipresence of the Internet. Consumer expectations have also changed to match the technology. Today, we want our needs met not only quickly but also in a variety of ways. If a company can't do that, the newly spoiled consumer will seek another provider. The second and perhaps most obvious change is that Prudential is now clearly a global enterprise. Ever since John

SHERRY MEIER

We are not working in an environment where the boss comes out in the morning and says, "This is what we are going to do today," and everybody says, "Yes, sir," and runs to their desk and gets it done.

You are challenged on everything at every level by everyone—by your peers, your staff and the customers.

So you really need to be on top of things and stay on your toes. It creates a more inclusive, cooperative atmosphere. You work together with your clients to figure out what is best for them. You work together with the group and staff to figure out the best way to get the job done. And that is a positive thing.

Sherry Meier, Dresher, Pennsylvania

Opposite: A sales champion at Prudential of Korea, Oujin Hwang instills in his trainees the need for a team-oriented sales force whose members help one another meet or exceed their goals. *Below:* Hwang brings trainees together weekly to discuss their experiences, how they are honing their skills and the importance of a positive mental attitude.

Dryden opened Prudential's second branch in Paterson, New Jersey, the company has always sought to keep its competitive edge through growth and expansion. In earlier years, the company depended upon traditional avenues provided by America's growing population and increased wealth. But those avenues now reach around the world. Technology has enabled any company—including, of course, Prudential—to bring its goods and services to new markets abroad. But the "new" global Prudential continues to do what it has always done—maintain its preeminence by developing new products, finding new customers and serving them well.

A third factor has had an enormous influence not only on Prudential but also on every similar institution in America: the changing nature of the financial services industry. Robert Winters put it very well: "When I started with Prudential in the

Back in 1971 as a young agent in Kentucky, I was in the life underwriters training program. The assignment was to go out and talk to two business people in the community. I chose Colonel Harlan B. Sanders. He had a restaurant in Shelbyville. Every day at noon, he came to the restaurant and walked by every table, asking customers how everything was. When he came by my table, I asked if I could speak with him. He said to come find him out on the porch. After dinner, I found the colonel sitting in a rocking chair.

"Son, what is it you want to talk about?"

"Your insurance, Colonel Sanders."

He looked at me kind of funny. "Who do you work for?" I told him Prudential.

He said, "I worked for Prudential for one week when I lived in the eastern Kentucky mountains. However, I didn't have a car so I couldn't get around and so I couldn't work for them. But that's OK because I went off and got this fried chicken thing going."

Denny Axman, Jacksonville, Florida

Agents carried collection books to record monthly premiums when they called on policyholders. Agent George P. Weber of the Beardstown, Illinois, office used this collection book in 1933 and 1934.

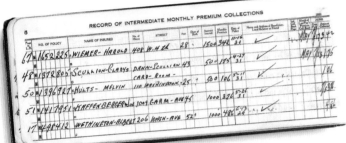

early 1950s, individual life insurance for a mutual life insurance company was a fairly easy business that can be oversimplified by saying, 'Make sure that you are charging a premium which is big enough, try to run the place reasonably effectively and give back the money you don't spend.' This is not a hard paradigm. But the business changed enormously in the 40 years that I was around."

As early as the chairmanship of Donald MacNaughton in the early 1970s, financial institutions have faced increasing competitive pressure to be more comprehensive—to be, if not necessarily bigger, at least something more than they once were. Consequently, the past quarter-century has seen the emergence of two parallel trends: the gradual blurring of the distinction between banks, insurance companies and brokerage houses and the rise of an increasing number of large, comprehensive financial services institutions. The latter factor has,

First application received by The Prudential Friendly Society, November 10, 1875.

Not to be filled } No. 1
in by the Agent.

ADULT APPLICATION.

THE PRUDENTIAL FRIENDLY SOCIETY,

NEWARK, N. J.

DECLARATION TO BE SIGNED BY THE APPLICANT.

I declare that the answers to questions Nos. 1 to 20 inclusive, hereinafter stated, are strictly correct, and that I have withheld no material information. I agree that those answers and this statement shall be the basis of the contract between me and THE PRUDENTIAL FRIENDLY SOCIETY for securing the benefit herein applied for, and which, if granted, shall be on terms contained in such Certificate of Membership, as shall be issued in pursuance of this Application. And when such Certificate shall be issued I agree to conform to the rules and regulations of the said Society, which are now or may hereafter be established.

Witness _John F. Dryden_   Signature of Applicant _Wm R Drake_

15   Dated this 10th day of Nov 187 5

What is your full name ?	Wm R Drake
Where do you live ?	Newark N J
What is your occupation ?	Banker
What is your age next birthday ?	30.—
What is your height and weight ?	5 feet, 8 inches, 122 lbs.
Are your Father and Mother both living ?	Yes
If living, what is their health ? If dead, state age at death ?	Fair
Are you now and have you always been sober and temperate ?	Yes.—
9. Are you now in sound health ?	Yes
10. Do you usually enjoy sound health ?	Yes
11. How long since you have been sick or consulted with a Physician as to your health ?	Never

The application of Prudential's first policyholder, William R. Drake, November 10, 1875.

Writing the First Policies

As with any start-up company, Prudential in its first months lavished great attention on every new sale. The story of how the first policies were counted in the fall of 1875 and the winter of 1876 is told by office boy, Carl August Giese, in *The Prudential: A Story of Human Security*, written for Prudential's 75th anniversary by Earl Chapin May:

"At that time applications came in very slowly. ... I can remember the pleasure of Dr. Ward in keeping tabs on the number when I brought the applications on odd days to his office on Walnut Street for his OK as medical director. ... He always used a blue pencil in affixing his initials, LDW. So also was Mr. Dryden pleased when I laid the finished policies on his desk for signature — the policies then were signed in longhand by the president and the secretary, but the writing of his name proved irksome to him. It was his custom to have me stand at his side to blot his signature as he finished it in his cramped handwriting, and often the perspiration stood out on his forehead before the tenth policy was signed."

naturally, increased competition among all such entities. Prudential's role within this movement has been significant. Beginning with the acquisition and development of its investment and securities unit in the early 1980s, the company didn't simply follow suit, but led.

Prudential has always been a work in progress and will remain so. The company's dynamism makes the writing of its most recent history particularly challenging. While the historian is looking back, the company is moving forward. We must for the moment be content to describe two dominant patterns that have characterized the past 25 years.

The first pattern emerged in the 1970s and continued into the early 1990s as Prudential grew into an enormous and highly diversified giant—a major presence in areas as diverse as health care, reinsurance, stocks and mutual funds, real estate ownership and insurance both here and abroad.

I once called on a distant cousin about life insurance. I didn't know that both he and his wife were deaf. They and their 7-year-old son communicated with sign language. "How do I begin this?" I thought.

The 7-year-old turned to me and said, "My dad wants a 10." I thought to myself, "Here's an obviously easy sale."

I said to the 7-year-old, "Please ask your dad if I could take a few moments and do an analysis of your parents' insurance needs."

So the boy came back and said, "My dad just wants a 10." Finally, I talked them through an analysis of their mortgage balance, education plans for the son, etc. I was able to fund their total needs.

Later, my cousin died of a heart attack. I remember sitting there with the wife and son, saying, "Remember? This is the amount we earmarked for education, this is the amount we earmarked for your mortgage, and this is the amount we earmarked for ongoing living expenses."

During this period, Prudential cannot be portrayed as one culture but a set of several coexistent business cultures, each with its own trajectory, its own beginning, middle and, sometimes, end.

The second pattern emerged in the 1990s. Driven by both internal trauma and an acceleration of the external factors discussed above, the company "reunified" into a single culture. And while this one universal vision is an undeniable benefit to the company, its history cannot yet be written. Only the next five years can accurately define the historical significance of the previous five. What can be portrayed, however, are the forces at work and in motion today as Prudential moves into a new century.

Cause to Celebrate. From October 13 to 17, 1975, The Prudential Insurance Company of America celebrated its centennial with anniversary events held in almost every Prudential outpost in the

Six months later, I was in the same neighborhood and was early for an appointment, so I watched a Little League game, and there was the son, now 9 years old, playing second base. It struck me: Because of life insurance, that boy could stay in that home and have a quality upbringing. Today, he's in college, and it's being paid for.

Larry Andrews, Chicago, Illinois

The Dollar Guide helped agents show clients the importance of early planning for a child's education.

THE DOLLAR GUIDE

W.P. Lynch, C.L.U.

MOST FATHERS WANT TO PROVIDE THEIR CHILDREN WITH A GOOD EDUCATION.

If their income is stopped by death, they want to make certain that their children will be able to continue their schooling.

THAT'S WHY THEY SET UP AN EDUCATION FUND.

* 70% of the leading vocations and professions require a college education.

* A college education doesn't cost—it pays . . . the average college trained man during his lifetime earns $180,000 more than the high school graduate.

* A college education is important to your child's future. Will the money be available when your child is ready to go to college?

Today, a sound education is **essential to success**

world. At the home office in Newark, a luncheon featured popular dishes of the 1870s. While a barbershop quartet entertained in the lobby of the Plaza Building, bonneted waitresses and gartered waiters served guests. Keystone Kops dashed around games of pin the tail on the donkey. Beaming mothers entered their offspring in baby contests while folks made a jolly mess of things in a pie-eating contest.

Indeed, Prudential had many reasons to

celebrate. The face of CEO Donald MacNaughton graced the cover of *Business Week*'s February 9 issue, and, within the past decade, Prudential had become the largest insurance company in America and, by some measures, the world. Prudential's assets were $4 billion larger than Metropolitan Life's and twice the size of third-ranked Equitable. On its 100th birthday, Prudential established new records in almost all areas of its operations. Life insurance sales

reached an all-time high of $30.8 billion in face amount sold. Life insurance in force jumped from $218.3 billion to $236.2 billion, another industry record—just like total assets, which rose from $35.8 billion to $39.3 billion. And Prudential's investment income was up $127 million to $2.22 billion.

Those barbershop quartets and bonneted servers were also reminders of how different the world had become. In 1975, disco was the dance craze as the Bee Gees celebrated *Stayin' Alive.* The world was cursed with the first of countless *Feelings,* while 26-year-old Bruce Springsteen claimed he was *Born to Run.* In October, America was introduced to *Saturday Night Live* and *A Chorus Line.* Beachside vacations became a little edgier after the world saw *Jaws* for the first time.

Advancing North Vietnamese forces forced Saigon to raise the white flag on April 30, ending America's most controversial and divisive war. At

DOROTHY WOLFE

My department was in charge of revising the rate books annually for both district and ordinary agencies. When I went to purchasing to get samples for the rate book covers, I would take them home and put them in my freezer and on the radiator to determine if they would crack or melt. That was for the agents in extreme climates like Canada and Texas because the agents would throw them in the trunk of their cars as they made their rounds.

I would come back to purchasing and say, "Oh, no. Look at this. I put it in the freezer and look what happened. We don't want this."

They used to think I was crazy, but I would say, "We get complaints from the agents."

One of the other things agents complained about that I had to be careful of is that covers had to be smooth and a little pliable. One lady sent in a claim because the agent scratched her dining room table with the spine of the rate book.

Dorothy Wolfe, Newark, New Jersey

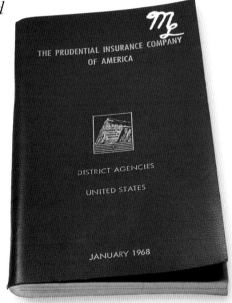

Rate books served as a quick reference tool, offering information on the various policies offered by the company.

home, Nixon cronies Mitchell, Haldeman and Ehrlichman donned prison garb for masterminding the Watergate break-in. Patty Hearst resurfaced, and Jimmy Hoffa didn't. A first-class stamp cost a dime. And, perhaps most portentous of all, a 19-year-old whippersnapper named Bill Gates founded Microsoft.

No Longer Just Insurance. In that period between barbershop and *Born to Run*, Prudential had changed a great deal, and it was now poised to continue to do so. As early as the late 1960s, Prudential's leaders felt that, to be competitive, the company must diversify beyond its more comfortable domain of life insurance. In doing so, Prudential was breaking new ground for the entire industry. According to the *Business Week* article, Prudential's decision to diversify was charting a new course that other big insurers would have to follow or risk losing more ground to the industry leader.

Donald S. MacNaughton: Founder of America's Corporate Conscience

ANTI-DEFAMATION LEAGUE OF B'NAI B'RITH

Prudential was established upon the need to give comfort and stability to the less fortunate, and that tradition has remained a part of the company throughout its history. Prudential's leaders have always played a major role in maintaining this legacy, but it was Donald S. MacNaughton, CEO from 1970 to 1978, who, responding to the social unrest of the late 1960s, formalized Prudential's civic and societal commitments and, in many ways, pioneered the notion of corporate social responsibility.

In his first speech to the Prudential President's Council after becoming president in 1969, he announced, "With stature comes responsibility. ... If ever it was proper to say our sole concern is Prudential and its people, it is no longer. If ever it was proper to say we are solely a business institution, not a social one, it is no longer."

Within the business community at the time, such sentiments were neither widespread nor popular. "Many companies just wanted to wait

MacNaughton, seen here in December 1974, frequently lent his time to speak to groups whose causes he supported.

September 1978 saw the retirement of Donald S. MacNaughton, Prudential's chairman and chief executive for the previous nine years. Under MacNaughton, Prudential had experienced great growth. Life insurance sales for 1968, the year before he became president, amounted to $13.5 billion. By 1977, sales had risen to $43.6 billion. In the same period, life insurance in force grew from $137.5 billion to $295 billion. Assets climbed from $26.6 billion to $46.3 billion. Much of that growth was the result of MacNaughton's wide-ranging program of diversification. At the time of his retirement in 1978, there were 14 Prudential subsidiaries.

Robert A. Beck succeeded MacNaughton after having served as Prudential's president since January 1974. Beck had been with the company for 27 years, starting as a part-time salesman while attending Syracuse University. He believed in salesmanship and the underlying values that out the social unrest and go back to the old patterns," MacNaughton explained recently. "They thought that curing social ills was the government's job." During this period, MacNaughton often spoke to business leaders about social responsibility, particularly about how companies could help improve life for the urban poor. "They gradually came over to my side," he said. But what prompted MacNaughton's convictions? "I believe that everybody should have an opportunity. I was a poor kid. I had nothing. But I was lucky to be 6-foot-4, so I became a basketball player and could go to college."

Under MacNaughton's leadership, Prudential formed a community affairs department, which, in turn, created The Prudential Foundation and other ongoing programs. With its own budget and professional staff, the department began a series of extraordinary social, educational and community service initiatives. These programs, in both scope and concept, established unprecedented partnerships between American business and society. Although these programs are now fashionable and increasingly widespread, Prudential created the model more than 25 years ago.

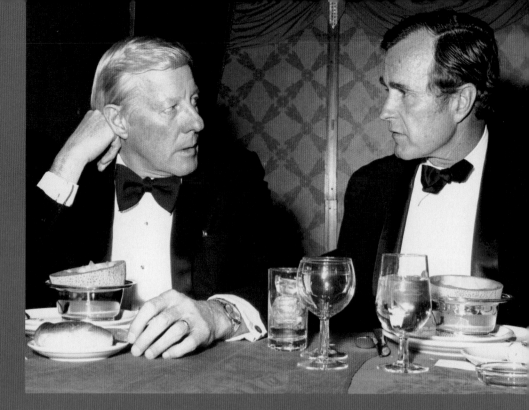

Above: Then-Director of the CIA George Bush listens to MacNaughton at a Harvard International Business Club Dinner, April 1976.
Left: MacNaughton speaks with Olympic decathlon gold medalist Milt Campbell in Newark.

create great salesmen and was given to maxims: "High achievers get there because they have high goals." "He is strongest who stands alone with the courage of his convictions." "Success is 15 percent aptitude and 85 percent attitude." He greatly admired the steadfastness and moral courage of Abraham Lincoln, of whom he was a conscientious student. Thus inspired, he inspired others. He was a motivator and role model for the Prudential agents who came in contact with him.

Beck's character, like his love of Lincoln, harkened back to an earlier era. His list of maxims was not unlike those hoarded by Horatio Alger's rags-to-riches heroes from 19th-century fiction. Yet, for all these qualities, Beck would hardly prove a traditionalist. One of his favorite maxims was "One must be prepared for the future." Beck, like the company itself, believed that constant values, of whatever era, must be wed to the changing demands of the present.

JOE GARZA

Prudential has always been a leader here in
the community. As part of the vice president's
Youth Motivation Task Force, we visited area
schools, concentrating on either the Hispanic
or black community. We would tell students
about the importance of graduating from
high school and going to college. We became
examples of members of the minority community able
to get good jobs at a place like Prudential.

But even before and in addition to that, many
of us had various places where we would volunteer our
time. I've always been able to volunteer, which is very
important to me.

Joe Garza, Woodland Hills, California

Consequently, Beck moved forward, continuing MacNaughton's program of diversification. By 1980, the Prudential umbrella sheltered 29 subsidiaries. Reinsurance operations had spread to Europe and Asia, and Prudential's health maintenance organization was expanding rapidly.

Vice Chairman Robert C. Winters became chairman of the board and CEO in February 1987, following Beck's retirement. Winters, like Beck, had joined the company in the early 1950s during its decentralization and had served as head of the Central Atlantic operations in the late 1970s before joining the executive office as executive vice president in 1978.

While Beck and Winters differed in personality and business focus—Beck having a grassroots sales background and Winters, a Yalie with a strong belief in innovation through business processes—their convictions regarding

both the operations and external direction of the company varied little. For example, one of the central purposes of Beck's reorganization in the early 1980s was to increase and clarify management accountability. Winters had already been working on what he termed "a fairly robust management accounting system" and continued to deal with the issue throughout his tenure.

Winters continued Prudential's current business strategies as well. Soon after assuming office, he declared, "Our answer to the challenges and uncertainties of the market remains the same: diversification. It is an answer that continues to serve us and our clients well." Therefore, the diversification initiated under MacNaughton and Beck continued to develop seamlessly and, in many cases, prospered under Bob Winters.

Offering the Customer More. The years immediately preceding the centennial had witnessed the introduction of two major

Since the earliest
days of the company,
Prudential has
committed itself to
supporting families
through tragic times.

Though death may enter there:
Though sorrow be your share,
It is much indeed when grief
Must be endured.
To think despite the blow,
How comforting to know
We are insured!"

I had sold a Variable Appreciable Life with a children's rider to a couple with two kids. Later, I learned that their youngest, 6 months old, had died. I didn't know how to handle going out and doing the death claim. When I was walking up the driveway to their house, I thought, "Please, God, get me through this."

We started the paperwork, and I was very professional. Then her 6-year-old son came in and said, "Mommy, when is my little sister coming back? Is this man bringing her back to us?" I looked at her, she looked at me, and we both lost it. We sat at the kitchen table for about 10 minutes hugging each other and crying. Afterward, I got in the car and thought, "What an idiot. You did everything you didn't want to do."

I visited the people again two years later, and the lady said, "You know what? You showed up at the right time. I needed someone to cry with. You were the guy."

I was there, and Prudential put me there. That's what we do.

Bob Satterfield, Mt. Laurel, New Jersey

subsidiaries: Prudential Property and Casualty, or PRUPAC, and Prudential Reinsurance, or Pru Re—both of which would experience great growth during the succeeding decade. These units were created by David J. Sherwood, a relative newcomer to the company but one whose talents were immediately obvious. Sherwood, who would later become president of Prudential, oversaw their quick expansion.

In PRUPAC, Sherwood saw a great opportunity to offer additional products to Prudential's life insurance customers. The unit began as a pilot project in Illinois in June 1971, and at the end of its first year, more than 22,000 policies had been issued. Three more states were added in 1972. Based upon their success, PRUPAC was introduced nationwide a year later. PRUPAC's growth through the '70s soon made it the largest of Prudential's subsidiaries. On its 10th anniversary in 1981, its staff had grown to

The 22 agents and 6 office
assistants of the Auburn, New York,
district office in 1917.

In Praise
of the Agent

The virtues and character of its agents
was taken seriously from the beginning
by Prudential. This excerpt from Elizur
Wright's Massachusetts Insurance Report
for 1863 was quoted in Frederick Hoffman's
*History of the Prudential Insurance
Company* (1900) and bears early witness
to Prudential's high expectations of the
quality of its agents.

"Forethought and mutuality of effort
to provide the most effectually against
future contingencies are not a spontaneous
growth of the human soil. It is a matter of
special cultivation; the result only of some
sort of missionary labor, nor withstanding
its manifest coincidence with the highest
interests of all concerned. ... Among the
honorable workers in the civilized world
to whom the public as well as the insured
will die indebted, we give faithful and
successful life insurance agents a high
place. ... It is hardly possible to believe
that a life insurance agent can achieve any
long-continued success without bringing
into action some of the noblest qualities
of a sterling man."

more than 4,000, and it ranked 12th in homeowners and 14th in private passenger auto coverage in the nation.

Pru Re started on June 13, 1973, with 17 employees and in its first year wrote $37 million in premiums. In its first 10 years, it grew into one of the world's leading reinsurers—fourth among U.S. reinsurers and ninth in the world.

Pioneering New Concepts in Health Care. Prudential had been directly involved in the operation of health maintenance organizations since it created PruCare in 1975. The company in many ways pioneered the concept. Its 1975 HMO in Houston was the first "group practice model" in the country. And on June 1, 1979, Prudential partnered with the Kaiser-Permanente Medical Care Program, then the world's largest nongovernmental health care delivery system, to create a vast HMO in Dallas, the first in the area.

Prudential's group health performance

I used to collect premiums from a woman named Pauline and later started to collect 5-cent premiums from her mother, Mary, who lived upstairs. Mary soon passed away. The claim was for $180. The policy—taken out in 1911—said on the bottom of the form that Prudential is a stock company. Well, I was new to the company so that didn't mean a whole lot to me. All I knew was that the policy didn't pay dividends. I didn't have the heart to tell Pauline, so I just went back to the office to complete the paperwork.

The check came, and I didn't bother to look at it because I knew it would only be for $180. I handed Pauline the envelope, and she began to cry. The check was for $1,700; she didn't have to mortgage her home to bury her mother. I later found out that when Prudential became a full mutual company, it credited all the old stock policies with the accumulated dividends and interest. That was my first death claim—and the highlight of my career.

Gerald Deridder, Iselin, New Jersey

flourished. Between 1982 and 1983, for example, HMO premium income rose 95 percent as membership increased by 50 percent, marking the third consecutive year of dramatic growth for the subsidiary. In 1985, PruCare celebrated its 10th anniversary by opening new divisions in North Carolina, Missouri and Ohio. With these additions, PruCare had 17 divisions and had become the nation's second-largest HMO operator.

Meanwhile, Prudential's life insurance and related units also continued to do well despite high interest rates and unemployment through the early 1980s. In 1982, total new premiums had reached $2.5 billion, a 25-percent increase over 1981. Total annuity sales reached nearly $1 billion, more than doubling the 1981 figure. New premiums for group insurance topped $1 billion for the first time, including the sale of the largest group creditors life case in Prudential's history, the Oregon Department of Veterans

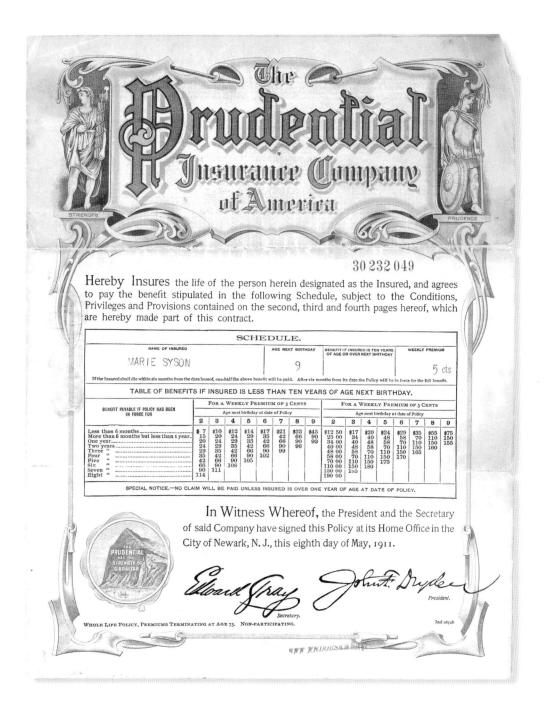

In 1911, Prudential's policies numbered 10,282,484, covering an astounding insurance amount of $2,018,499,340. For five cents a week, working-class families could afford insurance coverage that was once available only to the wealthy.

Affairs mortgage insurance account, which had $3.8 billion of group credit coverage and annual premiums of $24 million.

A Model for Overseas Expansion. Certainly the most daring move for Prudential was overseas. Globalization was hardly a household word in the mid-1970s, particularly for the insurance business. Therefore, when the company began market surveys in Japan in the fall of 1977, it raised more than a few eyebrows. Almost without exception, experts contended that an American-style product and marketing system wouldn't work there.

Cynics cited, among many other things, the difficult staffing issue. In Japan, insurance policies were almost exclusively sold by part-time female employees, often war widows, in a style that closely resembled door-to-door household-product sales. To realize Prudential's far more innovative and complex vision would require

educated, full-time professionals. But Prudential wisely ignored the experts. Company research indicated that, while 95 percent of Japanese households were already insured with an average of five policies apiece, the Japanese were nonetheless underinsured. Furthermore, while it was common knowledge that the Japanese were notoriously thrifty, the company discovered that much of the average Japanese family's assets were held in simple low-interest saving accounts. Not only could Prudential offer families an affordable and useful product, it could also provide a greater return on their investment.

To ease its entry into the Japanese market, Prudential partnered with Sony, which could provide needed expertise and experience in marketing and political procedures. On April 1, 1981, the Sony-Prudential Life Insurance Company opened four sales offices in metropolitan Tokyo.

Horror in Halifax

During World War I, 1,729 Prudential employees served in the armed forces and 50 gave their lives to the cause of battle. However, as William Carr wrote in his 100-year history of Prudential, not all the employees who stayed home escaped tragedy: "During World War I, Prudential civilians had to deal with death and maiming on a mass scale, too, after a munitions ship bound for Europe collided with another vessel in the harbor at Halifax, Nova Scotia, caught fire, and exploded with a noise heard 61 miles away. Two square miles of the city were totally destroyed, more than 1,600 men, women, and children were killed, and upwards of 4,000 persons were injured. There were so many Prudential policyholders among the victims that John H. Glover, the company's local manager, couldn't handle the job alone, so he appealed to the Home Office for help. The assignment was given to Albert C. Joyce ... and he sped from Boston to the Canadian city. For the rest of his

life he was haunted by the scenes of horror—the endless piles of debris, the bodies still buried under the rubble, the shocking wounds suffered by so many, the lack of shelter for the survivors and the rescue workers in the midst of a Canadian snowstorm, the threat of typhoid."

Today, the Halifax disaster is remembered as part of the Boston Tree Lighting. In 2001, Prudential celebrated its 30th anniversary as a sponsor. The ceremony is crowned by the lighting of a tree donated by the city of Halifax, in gratitude for the assistance given them by the people of Boston—such as Albert Joyce—whose generous donations and personal assistance helped Halifax through its tragic time.

Opposite: Family, friends and neighbors pay their respects to victims of the Halifax disaster. *Above:* A Halifax resident stands in the Richmond district, devastated by the explosion.

Prudential knew it had the right product, but it had not solved the difficult issues of staffing and marketing. In response, two precepts formed the foundation of Prudential's thinking in Japan: first, "Life insurance as a solution, not a product"; second, "Don't try to be the biggest, just the best." The company based every decision in Tokyo on these two ideas.

Prudential's recruiting and training program in Japan was radical and massively successful. Its

final version became a model for all subsequent overseas insurance ventures. It made no sense to recruit existing Japanese insurance personnel and reindoctrinate them in a totally new vision of the business. A quality sales force would have to be assembled from scratch, requiring Prudential to recruit college graduates with no experience in life insurance. Next, to distinguish its new recruits from mere "salespeople," they would be called "life planners," thus reinforcing their

Above: Takashi Matsumoto chats with a customer while on his way to visit his middle school alma mater to introduce the Spirit of Community program in 1997.
Opposite: Executive Life Planner Motokazu Saiga, Shibuya Agency, discusses policy details with the Murayama family in their home.

Last December, a customer, a 32-year-old single man, contacted me. He had been diagnosed with cancer and would probably not live through May. However, his parents felt that if there were even a 1 percent chance of survival, they would try anything.

His insurance had a Living Needs Benefit, which would permit him to take the money out while still alive. His mother said, "If we take this money, we are acknowledging that our son's death is near; but we will be eased of the burden of the monthly medical bill." Her sentiments were in conflict, but she thanked me with tears in her eyes.

Last month, this man passed away. At his funeral service, his boss gave a eulogy in which he told of visiting the young man in the hospital. He asked his boss, "Is there any game in life in which a loser can be made whole again?" The boss responded, "You are not a loser in life. You are a winner at fighting disease, a winner in life."

Takashi Matsumoto, Tokyo, Japan

expertise in needs-based selling as well as their role as counselors. Becoming a "life planner" required every bit of the legendary Japanese work ethic. The training regimen, developed over several years, was daunting. In its final version, sales managers went through nine hours of instruction a day, six days a week, for two months, after which they moved on to 10 weeks of on-the-job sales training before returning for two more months in the classroom. For the first time in Japan, Prudential was offering a custom-made insurance plan with schooled and dedicated professionals determining the individual needs of each customer. Everybody won. The customer got a great product, and agent retention in Japan became the highest in the business.

The Sony-Prudential operation exceeded its sales goals within its first five weeks of operation. By 1987, Sony-Prudential had nearly 51,000 individual life policies in force along with

substantial amounts of group business. That same year, Prudential bought out the partnership to form a wholly owned life insurance subsidiary on the islands. By changing the way insurance was conceived and sold in Japan, Prudential had not only established a firm foothold overseas, but it had also created a model for further overseas expansion.

Taking the Lead in Financial Services. By 1981, CEO Bob Beck knew that an essential weapon was missing from Prudential's arsenal: a window on Wall Street. Few insurers had tried to expand into the brokerage business, and none had succeeded, but Prudential was willing to take the chance. On June 12, 1981, after what Prudential executives described as "the longest board meeting in the Pru's history," Prudential announced its $385 million acquisition of Bache Halsey Stuart Shields Inc., the nation's sixth-largest brokerage and investment banker.

DENIS UNDERKOFFLER

*W*hen we first started Prudential Real Estate, we had a health and life insurance program for our affiliates and their salespeople, even though, as contractors, they aren't employees of Prudential.

An individual called me and explained that her brother had been a salesperson for Prudential Real Estate and had contracted AIDS and was unable to work. She felt that the benefits that he had with us had not been handled properly. In fact, his life insurance had been cancelled. I made some inquiries. After a series of calls, Prudential ended up saying we didn't handle the cancellation correctly and reinstated this individual's life insurance.

Some months later, I got a note from this person's mother saying that he had passed away, but that the family, who spent a lot of money on his health care, was able to survive because of his life insurance. It was one of the most fulfilling things I've ever been involved with.

Denis Underkoffler, Irvine, California

Prudential volunteers have donated their time and efforts to raising money for and coordinating displays of the AIDS Memorial Quilt around the nation. In June 2001, Prudential hosted its first major display of the quilt in several of its office locations in the East and Midwest.

The Bache acquisition took Wall Street by surprise. Not only would it take Prudential into direct competition with Merrill Lynch and other brokerage firms, it would also be a merger of unlikely partners. Overnight, the cynical eye of Wall Street—not to mention of the ever-cautious insurance industry—was trained on the product of this union: Prudential-Bache Securities.

Bache, at 102 years old, was one of the oldest, largest and best-known investment brokerage firms in the world. The company was established in 1879 by German immigrant Leopold Cahn, who was joined a year later by his nephew, Jules S. Bache. Jules took ownership soon thereafter, reorganizing and renaming it J.S. Bache & Co., which he ran until his death in 1944. By 1896, the company supported full-time correspondents in London and Paris. Among its early clients were such renowned financial leaders as John D. Rockefeller Sr., Edward H. Harriman and Jay

GERALD KUSCHUK

Bache was going through tough times in 1983. We felt like a few chickens surrounded by a bunch of foxes. But when Prudential bought Bache, we could not think of a better buyer. It was like we now had a big lion to scare away all the foxes that were chasing us. The other guys backed off. It was very uplifting at the time.

In 1987, we had the stock market crash, and some firms did not survive.

In those days, everything was in turmoil—everything was going up in smoke. We felt good, though, because Prudential told us, "We're still here for you."

They were there for us in '83, and they were there for us in '87. We've been through a lot of tough times, and Prudential was always here behind us.

Gerald Kuschuk, New York, New York

Prudential acquired the Bache Group, Inc. on March 19, 1981. Attending the contract signing were (from left, standing) Garnett L. Keith Jr., senior vice president, Prudential Corporate Finance Department; H. Virgil Sherrill, president Bache Group, Inc.; (from left, seated) Robert A. Beck, chairman and CEO, Prudential; and Harry A. Jacobs Jr., chairman and CEO, Bache.

Gould. At the time of its sale to Prudential, Bache's capital was $179 million, with 3,400 account executives among 7,300 total employees in 230 offices in the United States and 18 other countries.

With its expansion into financial services, Prudential was clearly blazing an attractive trail. Through its acquisition of Bache, Prudential could offer its 50 million customers an established line of investment-oriented products and services and expand into new personal investment areas without incurring heavy product-development costs. The consolidation quickly became a model for other companies. Three other takeovers quickly followed: American Express' $950 million purchase of Shearson Loeb Rhoades, Philbro's $250 million acquisition of Salomon Brothers and Sears' $500 million takeover of Dean Witter Reynolds.

Many thought that a vast insurance company

Ward Saves the Company

Dr. Leslie D. Ward, one of Prudential's first investors, prevented a claim with the prompt treatment of a client. On a February afternoon in 1876, Prudential founder John Dryden told the doctor of a Mrs. Grover, insured for $500, who had pneumonia and would not survive the night. Earl Chapin May relates in his 1950 history, *The Prudential: A Story of Human Security,* that Mrs. Grover's life was not the only one Ward saved, according to the doctor's account: "'Mr. Dryden and I both realized that a claim of $500 at that particular time would very likely wreck the company. The only way to save the company was to save Mrs. Grover. And this I endeavored to do.' He went to the home, raised her in the bed so she could breathe better, applied poultices, and administered stimulants. 'It was not only a case of keeping the policyholder alive—which I am delighted to say that I succeeded in doing—it was also a case of keeping the balance of the Grover family and myself from freezing to death. The fire in the stove kept going out. I found I had to "treat" that fire as regularly as I treated the patient. It was a long, cold night.'"

The Prudential Friendly Society.

Div. 19 1 0 Pd. 12-19-10

No. 104

This Certificate of Membership Witnesseth: That THE PRUDENTIAL FRIENDLY SOCIETY, in consideration of the representations and agreements, made to and with them, in the application therefor, and of the sum of money stated in column No. 2 of the schedule embodied herein, to them in hand paid, and of a like sum to be paid, on or before the *First* Monday of every *June + December* succeeding the date hereof, during the life-time of the person named and described in column No. 1 of said schedule, have constituted said person a member of said Society; and the said Society hereby promises and agrees to and with the said member as follows, to wit:

After satisfactory proof of the decease of said member, the said Society will pay unto the person or persons designated in the answer to question number twenty contained in the application for this certificate, or to his, her or their executors or administrators, the amount mentioned on line A in column No. 3 of said schedule.

Above: The Prudential Friendly Society membership certificate of Isabella Grover. *Opposite:* (from left) Prudential President John F. Dryden with Vice Presidents (and brothers) Edgar and Dr. Leslie D. Ward on Dryden's yacht *Alcedo,* September 1903.

and a Wall Street brokerage house were improbable partners. As one Prudential insider put it, "The brokerage business is an in-office telephone business while insurance offices are empty all day as agents make personal calls." Others cited the uncomfortably divergent thought processes inherent in the two institutions. Insurers were, as they said, "slow and analytical" while brokerages depended on "quick decisions."

But diverse personalities often make good marriages. And upon such hope—and forethought—Prudential set about to make Prudential-Bache a fruitful union. After all, it had much to offer. In addition to an enormous customer base, Prudential also boasted a $67 billion balance sheet, which would allow Prudential-Bache (so renamed in October 1982) to plan long term without the traditional brokerage house fretting over Wall Street's inevitable gyrations. Prudential also brought a

century of experience managing large amounts of both money and people. Likewise, Bache's dowry was not small. In addition to about 738,000 upscale customers ranging from individual investors to institutions and corporations, Bache brought its name, terrific marketing skills and a greater familiarity with sophisticated technology.

Within months, Prudential-Bache was offering its customers new, innovative products, many of them first-of-their-kind financial services. For example, the Bache Command Account was first offered in April 1982 and, unlike traditional brokerage accounts, allowed its customers to write checks on their margin accounts and use debit cards allied with a money market mutual fund. From an end-of-the-century perspective, such an offering might not seem like much. It is, therefore, startling to realize that Prudential-Bache's Command Account was among the first of its kind anywhere. Prudential's early

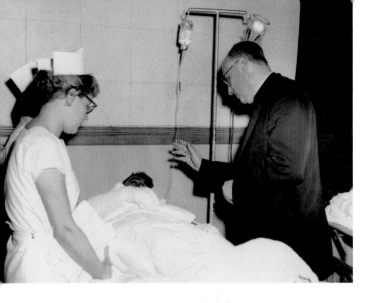

Ninety-eight children and nuns died as a result of a fire that raged through Our Lady of the Angels School on December 1, 1958. The fire revealed severe problems in fire safety standards in schools and paved the way for reform across the nation.

BRUNO PINKOS

I was the manager of the North Austin District in Chicago. It was the first of December, and the Fire Department was coming down the street. Little did we realize that the Our Lady of the Angels School was on fire. Over 90 children lost their lives. Prudential said to me, "Bruno, we want to give with our hearts." I went to the wakes, the funerals and the homes. We paid claims without death certificates. This was Prudential in action. Prudential is great. It is not a thing. It is not a spirit. It is human beings.

Bruno Pinkos, Chicago, Illinois

efforts in "one-stop financial shopping" were also the first for the financial services industry.

Prudential knew that taking a risk on an original product came with the burden of leadership. The entire enterprise would demand the fearlessness of an entrepreneur, perhaps odd casting for a company of Prudential's age and stature, but a role that Prudential was willing to take. In adding a securities and investments capability, Prudential knew it was in uncharted territory. No model existed for how best to integrate the two entities. As with other Prudential ventures of the time—Prudential of Japan being an apt example—the company would have to create its own model. And it had, like any good explorer, to be willing to blaze several trails up the mountain before finding the right one.

Among Prudential's first moves was enabling brokers and agents to sell each other's products.

Nearly 5,400 of Prudential's 23,000 agents became registered with the National Association of Securities Dealers. Nationwide sales of eight Bache mutual funds began in October 1982. On the other side, Bache account executives began marketing PRUFLEX, Prudential's newest annuity product.

Such efforts, however, failed to provide Prudential-Bache with a coherent direction and a clearly defined relationship with Prudential. The marriage also had to struggle through what *The Wall Street Journal* called "a sickening slide in stock prices and anemic trading volume." After the unit reported a $49.4 million loss in the first half of 1982, Prudential quickly brought in George Ball, then president of E.F. Hutton, and to provide much needed continuity and advice, Prudential retained the unpretentious and genteel Harry Jacobs as chairman and Virgil Sherrill as vice chairman of the new subsidiary, both of

In 1970, I was hired into a pretty forward-thinking program as a computer programmer. At the time, there weren't very many computer science majors so Prudential was the training ground. The idea behind Prudential's program was to provide training for programmers and develop managers to go out to the rest of the organization and address the fear of automation.

You can track the development of my career through the development of the computer. One of the very first things I did with the company was to go to a class on the old 705. The computers obviously got smaller and smaller and more and more powerful. For many years, we were main-frame based. It wasn't really until 1983 or so that personal computers came onto the scene. They were expensive. I'm sure that what we all have sitting on our desks today is much more powerful than the biggest computer in the computer room on the day I started.

Angie Mann, Dresher, Pennsylvania

Above: Laptop computers have become a part of everyday work for many at Prudential, such as Conor McDermott of Prumerica Systems Ireland Limited. *Opposite:* After three years of planning and preparation by hundreds of employees, the IBM Model 705 was introduced in 1958.

whom were well-respected fixtures within the Wall Street community. Jacobs had spent his entire professional life at Bache, starting in its research department in 1946. Sherrill, a tall and gentlemanly former Navy fighter pilot, came up through the banking side of the business and was president and CEO of Shields Model Roland when that company joined Bache.

Ball acted quickly. By November 1982, he had overseen a wholesale reorganization of the firm. The restructured management was peopled by executives Ball recruited from Hutton, including its chief economist and key people in research and investments. He had reorganized Prudential-Bache's research department and hired four institutional traders from Hutton to bring depth to a business in which Bache had been weak. Ball also had added 15 offices in the United States, three in Canada and three new international branches, which put the total

number of offices at 240 in 17 countries.

Efforts to cross-sell continued. By June 1983, more than half of the 23,000 Prudential agents had some form of security licensing. By the end of the year, Prudential-Bache had joint insurance-brokerage operations at 30 locations around the country. "Prudential-Bache has been reaping the rewards for about a year and a half from its cross-selling efforts of the insurance force," *Securities Week* noted. "Prudential-Bache's tax-managed utility, high-yield corporate bond, high-yield municipal bond and equity funds are popular products with Prudential agents." Yet, as *The Economist* also reported, the joint sales operation was far from a bust-out success: "Of the $11.6 billion in mutual funds sold by Prudential-Bache in 1983, little more than $100 million were sold by its army of life insurance salesmen. Prudential and Bache found that their brokers and insurance agents needed a long, formal introduction. ...

Joseph Melone, president of Prudential from 1984 to 1990, meets with former First Lady Rosalynn Carter at the Prudential Foundation's 10th anniversary celebration in Newark in 1988.

My brother-in-law Morty was an agent. He went on disability with Lou Gehrig's disease. When I visited him 2 years later, he told me, "Rosalee, I have a mission for you."

Joe Melone was president of Prudential and he knew Morty. Morty said, "I want you to speak to Joe because with Lou Gehrig's disease you wind up on a respirator. I want to know that Prudential will be behind me and pay for the nursing care—you need 24-hour care when you're on a respirator."

I called Joe and told him about Morty and that the time was coming to decide whether he would go on a respirator. Morty's family was used to a good lifestyle, and he did not want to take from them to pay for his care.

Joe said, "Tell Morty to get the respirator. We're family at Prudential. We care about him."

Morty went on the respirator, and Prudential continued paying. With enormous help from Prudential, Morty died with dignity.

Rosalee Zodikoff, West Caldwell, New Jersey

Synergy, if it works at all, works slowly."

So, as the company entered 1984, while bold and decisive moves had been taken, the question of Prudential-Bache's ultimate identity was yet to be answered. For Ball, even bolder moves—for better or worse—lay ahead.

Expanding Financial Services Here and Abroad. During the 1980s, Prudential expanded its role as investor, particularly in real estate. For example, in early 1982, in what might have been the largest single real estate sale in the United States, Prudential paid $530 million for an 80 percent interest in Denver's City Center, a four-block office and hotel complex in the Mile-High City's downtown. The purchase, made for PRISA, Prudential's Property Investment Separate Account, was one of many that made the company, by 1985, among the largest developers in the country.

Meanwhile, the mid-1980s saw Prudential

B E L L A   L O Y K H T E R

I am from Russia, where I got my education in computer science. When I came to the United States, I did not even know what a brokerage company was. I had an interview with Bache, and they offered me a job. After a couple of weeks with Bache, my boss sent me to a meeting.

My English at that time was very rough and definitely needed improvement. The man at the meeting spoke so fast that I could not make out a word of what he was saying. I tried to concentrate, but pretty soon, I started asking myself why I was even there, and tears started gathering in my eyes. I was scared because I did not know what was going on.

When the speaker sensed my confusion, he said to me, "Don't worry; I will help you out. I will speak very slowly until you definitely understand." I feel like that caring and helpful attitude really describes my 23-year experience with Bache and Prudential.

Bella Loykhter, New York, New York

Inside the offices of Prudential Securities—formerly Prudential-Bache—colleagues consult frequently, creating an environment of constant learning.

extend its brand name into the global financial services market, particularly in Asia. Prudential Asset Management Asia was established in 1986 to provide fast-growing, established businesses through the Pacific region with long-term equity capital. Headquartered in Hong Kong, the subsidiary was soon investing in 12 countries and in such disparate holdings as a prominent Hong Kong film production and distribution group, a food company that markets instant noodles in China and a fast-growing Malaysian manufacturer of surgical rubber gloves. By 1989, the unit's investments were valued at more than $650 million.

Responding to "a Changed World." While Prudential benefited from its program of diversification during the late 1970s and early 1980s, its insurance sales were being hit hard from several angles. Severe inflation and high interest rates made it difficult to convince consumers that whole life insurance—

GIBRALTAR NEWS

Vol. 3, No. 14
Dec. 7, 1956

THE PRUDENTIAL INSURANCE COMPA
NORTH CENTRAL HOME OFFICE, MINNE

An Unwelcome Houseguest

William Carr wrote in the book *From Three Cents a Week* ... about a visit Frank Lloyd Wright paid to Prudential: "The famous architectural genius and curmudgeon had been invited to lecture to a local cultural society. When he arrived in Minneapolis in November 1956, little more than a year after the official opening of NCHO's building, his hosts took him on a tour of some of the architectural sights in the area. One of the first stops was the new Pru building. [Vice President and head of the North Central Home Office Orville] Beal greeted him at the door. What happened during the next few minutes must have strained even the tolerance of Beal, whose patience usually seemed inexhaustible.

"Emerging from the car, Wright, then 87 years old and a colorful sight in a brown tweed coat with a high collar, wearing a shaggy felt hat which could not quite contain his bushy mane, looked about him, eyed the new building dyspeptically, and snorted, 'To build a thing like this in a park is my idea of a poetry crusher with a capital P.'

Above: Frank Lloyd Wright (left) tours the North Central Home Office in 1956 with Orville E. Beal (right), then Vice President of the Minneapolis office.
Opposite: The North Central Home Office, ca. 1955.

Prudential's bread and butter—offered them the benefits and protection they desired. Instead, many potential customers were investing in money market funds and individual retirement accounts or experimenting with a host of new insurance products that separated savings from protection and tied yields to current money rates. When they bought life insurance, they bought term. Inflation also prompted a $52 million loss in automobile and homeowners insurance in 1981,

and the individual and small group health operations suffered back-to-back deficits: $9 million in 1982 after an '81 loss of $286 million. With Prudential-Bache still gaining its sea legs and struggling with a sluggish Wall Street, something had to be done.

While the solution was still unclear, Beck knew it should be more than a tweak. In January 1982, Beck announced that Jack Kittredge, then Prudential's executive vice president, would head

"The most cutting blow of all came in the cafeteria, where Wright looked about him and commented, 'I wouldn't gather from this that you really love your employees.' It wasn't that he didn't like anything. He expressed approval of the escalators. And in the kitchen he delivered a pat and a kick: 'This kitchen is well done—an example of how far we have come with our civilization. Go out in front of this building and you see where we've failed.'

"Just before he got into his car to leave, Wright cast a parting stone: 'This whole thing is a misadventure.'

"That must have been just the word Beal would have used to describe Wright's visit.

"None of the original critics of the Pru's building could have taken much comfort from the great architect's comments. In the course of his subsequent tour of the city he managed to flay Minneapolis because of a number of other local landmarks. Before departing from the city, he advised Minneapolitans to tear down the whole city and start all over— advice he had previously given to New York City and any number of other places large and small."

up the Strategic Planning and Organization Task Force along with its full-scale examination of the company's organization and future development. As Beck noted later, "There were no sacred cows, no accepted assumptions, no boundaries to their explorations." Kittredge's final report, the Strategic Planning and Organization Study, called for an aggressive reorganization of the company, the most drastic element of which was a consolidation of the regional home offices and a

subsequent shift of personnel.

Beck announced the reorganization on July 12, 1983, to management in Newark. Over 18 months, the individual life, property and casualty, and small group insurance operations would be consolidated from eight into four regional home offices: Jacksonville, Florida; Fort Washington, Pennsylvania; Minneapolis, Minnesota; and Los Angeles, California. Smaller regional marketing offices that provided direction and support for the

House calls provide agents the opportunity to meet with clients in an environment where they feel most comfortable.

I once knew an agent who used to tell this story about a letter that came back to the agency. The recipient had written "Send No Salesman!" on it. The agent went to his manager and asked what he should do about the letter. The manager advised the agent to go see the man the next night around dinnertime because he knew that the man would be home.

The next night, the agent knocked on the door, and the man got up, obviously in the middle of dinner. The agent began to talk to the man through the screen door.

The agent said, "Sir, do you remember this letter?" holding it up to the screen so the man could see it.

The prospect said to the agent, "Can't you read this letter? I wrote on the bottom, 'Send No Salesman!'"

The agent replied, "Sir, I'm the closest thing to a 'No Salesman' that the agency's got!"

Merle Mattenson, Chicago, Illinois

individual agencies would remain in Boston, Chicago, Houston and northern New Jersey.

These were, undoubtedly, formidable changes. But the company had undergone such sweeping reorganizations before, most notably with its massive postwar decentralization. Beck's long service with the company gave him the perspective to realize that while these two movements—one an expansion, the other a contraction—appeared to contradict one another,

both were in fact accurate and timely responses to market pressures and new opportunities provided by technology. And most importantly, they were both designed to serve the customer better.

Beck emphasized from the beginning that while the moves were expected to produce annual savings of about $50 million, it was technology, not cost-cutting, that prompted the decision. Beck noted that marketplace pressures, particularly the rapid introduction of new and attractively priced

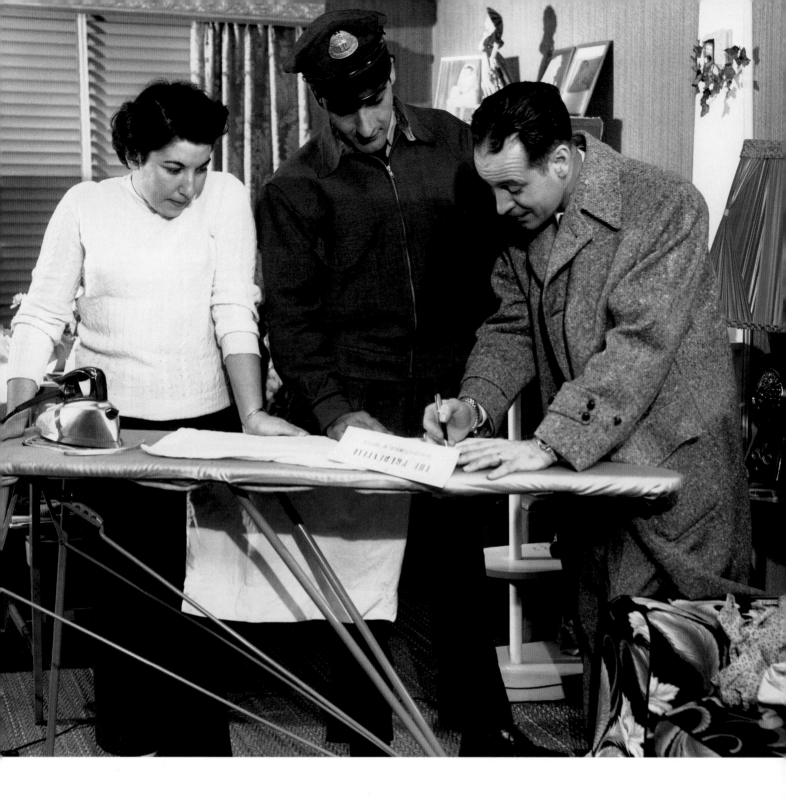

products from competitors, were also major factors. The consolidation would allow Prudential to contain cost increases in marketing and administration while reducing the time needed for research, technical development and the introduction of new products. Moreover, the involvement of the regional home offices in group insurance and other activities had distracted them from their primary mission: individual insurance operations. The strategy would also refocus management's attention on profitability by establishing clearer organizational missions and objectives and redefining lines of authority, responsibility and communication.

Beck, who himself began as a field agent, knew the reorganization was going to disrupt lives, but he was also certain the company had few alternatives. The plan, he said, "prepares us to succeed in a changed world." When asked about having to reduce the work force, he said, "I

I was on my third visit to a family. I knew the guy was going to buy, but I couldn't get him to sign. I tried all of the standard closes. "Sign the application. We can be evaluating you while you're evaluating us." We went through the medical and all those different closes that they teach you, and none of them were working.

I had arrived at 7 and was still there 10 at night. Finally, I said, "Mr. Jones, just sit back and relax. Have I ever showed you my magic tricks?" and, of course, he said no.

I was getting ready to start a trick when he said, "That's enough. I'll buy." So I pulled out the application, and he signed it.

When I delivered the policy, his married daughter was there with her child. When the man introduced me, he said, "Just fill out the application right now before he gets to the magic tricks."

Brian Murphy, Plymouth, Minnesota

Opposite: In 1953, the Insurance Salesman published a book of sales ideas said to be proven deal-closers. Salesmen from across the country wrote in and offered their colorful suggestions for everything from retirement planning to selling policies to farmers.

think this question is about a world that has disappeared."

By 1985, Prudential's changes—far-reaching and at times uncomfortable—began to pay off. New business premiums and considerations from sales of life and health insurance and annuity products nearly doubled from $5.5 billion in 1984 to $8.3 billion. The amount of individual life insurance sold went up 20 percent over the previous year, and individual and small group life and health insurance jumped a whopping 42 percent to $131 million.

The Strongest Line of Products Ever. One of the central purposes of Beck's consolidation had been to allow the company to focus less on operations and more on essential areas, not the least being new product development. In the three years after the announcement of the reorganization, the renewed focus began to show results.

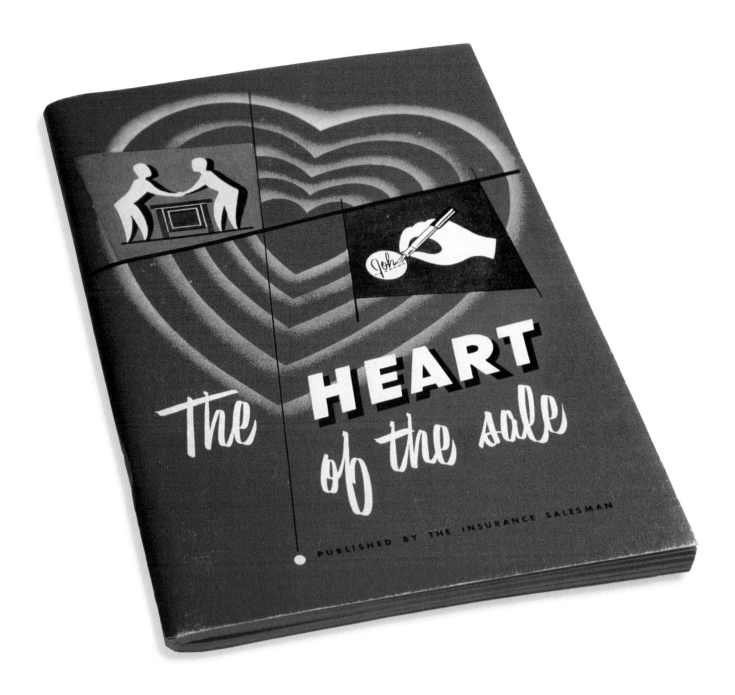

Inflation-sensitive customers were demanding more from their investments, and in the mid-1980s, Prudential responded with innovative offerings. In 1983, the company began selling a variable life insurance policy that offered policyowners the opportunity to allocate the policy's contract fund among three different investment funds: common stock, money market and bond. The new policy provided the valuable hedge against inflation that customers demanded.

The company followed up the next year with a new "life builder" policy, a permanent plan that earned interest at current market rates and was designed to compete with increasingly popular investment-oriented insurance products. In November 1984, agents began selling two new flexible premium products. Nationwide sales of the appreciable life policy began November 2, and the following week, sales of Variable Appreciable Life (VAL) began on a pilot basis in

Citizen-Soldier and Prudential's Sixth President: "Colonel" Franklin D'Olier

When Franklin D'Olier joined Prudential in 1926 as executive vice president, he was already serving as the president of his family's cotton business in Philadelphia, sitting on Princeton's board of trustees and, by his own admission, planning to retire soon. Luckily for Prudential, he was intrigued by the challenges this new position offered and from the beginning distinguished himself as President Edward Duffield's right-hand man. Twelve years later, D'Olier succeeded Duffield as the sixth president of the company.

Long before he joined the Pru, D'Olier had proven himself as a man unafraid of challenges. In World War I, he was sent to France to organize the salvage service for the American Expeditionary Force. His skills as an organizer and administrator were immediately put to a severe test. Funds and materiel were scarce. Everything possible had to be gathered, repaired or reworked and put back into service. He began with a staff of 6 but, within half a year, had 7,000 people working for him—all responsible for meeting the uniform needs of a million soldiers. At one point, he learned that the wounded had no hospital slippers and were forced to wear their combat boots—in bed and out. He located 100,000 discarded campaign hats, reworked them and had them in the field hospitals within weeks. He established another outpost in Lyon, France, where his charges repaired 10,000 pairs of shoes a day. Such efforts saved the American Expeditionary Force more than $23 million and earned D'Olier a Distinguished Service Medal and France's Legion of Honor. Upon returning from the war, D'Olier—by this time a colonel—became a founding member and the first national commander of the American Legion.

D'Olier took on the challenges at Prudential with similar verve. Duffield once complained to D'Olier's wife, "If Frank wants to work himself to death, that's his business, but why does he have to work me so hard?" As president, D'Olier's greatest contribution—and a feat not unworthy of his war efforts—was the final establishment of Prudential as a mutual insurance company.

Despite his military background, D'Olier was funny and self-deprecating. He once admitted, "I never prepared any speech. I would simply have about 10 points I wanted to cover, and if

the Northeast with national sales scheduled early the following year. The VAL initiative included a major breakthrough. Prudential was the first company to move toward having its life insurance agents fully registered and licensed to sell variable products.

With these interest-sensitive products featuring flexible premium payments, Prudential offered its customers yet more variety and responsiveness to the market while providing the tax benefits and guaranteed death benefits of other whole life products. Customers saw the value as well. More than 100,000 policies were sold in 1985, accounting for 21 percent of all new life premiums.

Prudential developed one of its most innovative and customer-sensitive products later in the decade: a living needs benefit rider. First offered by Canadian operations in the late 1980s and introduced in the United States in 1990, this

you and 10 other members of the family get no presents from me.'"

Yet, even while D'Olier was immersed in his duties at Prudential, the military wasn't through with him. In 1944, the secretary of war presented him with what had to be a formidable challenge: to assess the effectiveness of all bombing missions taking place during World War II. The job was far from busy work. Germany was still a juggernaut, and D'Olier's mission was to assist the Department of War in determining the most effective deployment of aerial bombardment. To help produce what became the United States Strategic Bombing Survey, D'Olier assembled 1,600 military and civilian statisticians, researchers and observers under his command. To ensure that his task force would be of no burden to the men in combat, he commandeered a fleet of planes and 600 vehicles. Poring through millions of combat reports and witnessing roughly 15 months of bombardments first-hand, both in Europe and the Pacific Theater, D'Olier's final report filled 208 volumes and was declared a masterpiece of analysis. At the completion of his assignment, Colonel Franklin D'Olier, citizen-soldier, was 68 years old. He retired as Prudential's president on January 1, 1946.

Above: D'Olier accepts an American flag made by women employed in the Army's salvage depot, July 4, 1918, in Tours, France. *Opposite:* President D'Olier addresses Prudential employees in 1943 at the company's third war loan drive gathering.

I covered 6 of them, I considered the speech to be complete." In an interview, he recalled, "I always gave my children cash for Christmas presents, but one year, my wife said, 'Why don't you give them presents instead? That's giving them something of yourself.' So, at the first dinner party we had after that, I announced the new system, and a deadly silence answered my statement. My son looked up and said, 'That's a lovely idea, and I appreciate the sentiment, but the moment you go off the cash basis,

option advanced payment of life insurance benefits when the insured was terminally ill, permanently confined to a nursing home or an organ transplant recipient.

New Synergies in Financial Services. As the omnibus financial services concept continued to develop in the '80s, Prudential determined that real competitive power came not just from acquiring and developing new individual units but in creating an interactive business relationship among them. The competitive impact of such linkages would quickly prove its worth by giving the customer an array of related products through a number of potential sources. Such logic stood behind the emerging relationships among Prudential Bank, Prudential Real Estate and Relocation, and the company's home mortgage unit.

Prudential Bank was created in 1983 when Prudential Capital and Investment Services

Feeding an army of Prudential employees required expert preparation, industrial-size equipment and massive quantities of supplies. Every year, scheduling began more than one month in advance of the company's Thanksgiving dinners.

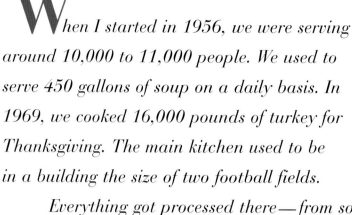

*W*hen I started in 1956, we were serving around 10,000 to 11,000 people. We used to serve 450 gallons of soup on a daily basis. In 1969, we cooked 16,000 pounds of turkey for Thanksgiving. The main kitchen used to be in a building the size of two football fields.

Everything got processed there—from soup to dessert. There was one room where we made ice cream with an enormous machine that had about 7,000 parts. It took a genius to put it together. They would ship the food to four different buildings. It was some operation. Everything was made in-house. It was essential that everything was very methodical and well-run to feed so many people. The schedule had to be followed, or else there would be long lines. And if you worked overtime, you got a hot fudge sundae.

Ray Ranucci, Newark, New Jersey

purchased the Capital City Bank of Hapeville, Georgia. The operation of the bank was then restructured to no longer accept checking and passbook savings accounts. Local assets were sold, and the bank was officially rechartered as the Prudential Bank and Trust Company. In 1984, Prudential Bank began marketing its first product— home equity loans—through Prudential-Bache financial advisers. Its first big liability product— jumbo CDs—expanded its consumer offerings that same year. By November 1985, Prudential agents were marketing Prudential Bank and Trust's regular certificates of deposit and money market deposit accounts. In 1987, Prudential Bank signed a contract with Signet Bank of Virginia to service the new Prudential MasterCard. That same year, bank assets surpassed $100 million, and the bank showed a profit of $100,000 for the year. By 1990, Prudential Bank served more than 200,000 customers in 50 states.

In 1985, after a 20-year absence, the company returned to the home mortgage market. Prudential took advantage of new technology by pilot-marketing innovative mortgage-by-telephone services in three states. In what was then a new concept, a customer could call a toll-free number, receive information about a Prudential mortgage and even apply for the mortgage without leaving home.

Under Bob Winters, Prudential's next step— the development of a vital and wide-ranging residential real estate component—linked these individual initiatives. Prudential Real Estate Affiliates, a network of franchised real estate offices, was formed in May 1988 and quickly expanded through the 1989 acquisition of Merrill Lynch's real estate franchises. PREA then boasted a network of nearly 900 offices with almost 25,000 sales associates in 39 states. After only three years of operation, Prudential Real Estate Affiliates was the fourth-largest residential

Prudential's farm and home mortgage business suffered during the Great Depression, but the company also did what it could to help those in need, as William Carr described in *From Three Cents a Week* ....

A Helping Hand During the Depression

"As the national economy ground almost to a halt, companies went bankrupt, people were thrown out of work, and millions could not meet their financial obligations. The Home Office and offices in the field were swamped with delinquencies. The flood of correspondence was so great that specialists had to be sent into various areas to work out problems on the spot.

"Whenever possible, the Pru tried to avoid foreclosure. The terms of mortgages were revised, or mortgages were extended, if there seemed to be any possibility of keeping the property in the hands of the mortgagors.

"In one—by no means rare—case, a Columbus, Ohio, home was purchased in 1927 and Prudential made a home loan on it. Time after time, the mortgage terms were eased or payments suspended to enable the couple who owned the house to get on their feet. It was not until 1937 that the family was able to resume regular payments.

"All over the country this sort of thing was going on with Prudential mortgages during the Depression.

To mark 50 years of farm lending, the Mortgage Loan & Real Estate Investment Department made a scrapbook of case histories from the Depression. Collected within its pages are the testimonials from 25 grateful farm loan recipients from South Dakota to Georgia.

real estate network in the country.

It quickly became a valuable part of a larger financial services network that Prudential had already set in place. The company saw an opportunity to serve its customers far beyond helping them buy or sell a house. Prudential could also provide homeowners insurance through PRUPAC, mortgage financing through the Prudential Home Mortgage Company, and home equity loans and credit cards through Prudential Bank and Trust.

Creating a vital real estate presence also offered an unanticipated benefit. No one knows a community like a real estate salesperson, and many of Prudential's 25,000 real estate affiliates quickly became ambassadors for the company and active participants in Prudential's growing number of community service initiatives.

Taking further advantage of these synergies, Prudential also created Prudential Relocation

In Lakeland, Florida, a railroad engineer was laid off, and for four years the Pru not only did not demand payments, but also even paid the taxes on the house. When the man was able to go back to work and resume payments, he wrote to the Pru, 'My family and I are certainly grateful to you for helping us keep a roof over our heads.'

"When farm mortgages were involved, the Prudential went to even greater lengths to help farmers keep their land. All representatives of the company were notified that it was the Pru's intention not to foreclose on any farm whose owner was making 'every effort in his power to meet his obligations.' If there were any possibility that the farmer could ultimately get on his feet, the Pru would abstain from foreclosure.

"Whether the mortgaged property was a farm or a home, if the Pru did have to foreclose, the company always gave the original owner preference—that is, the original owner could buy the property back for the amount of the mortgage or the market price, whichever was lower."

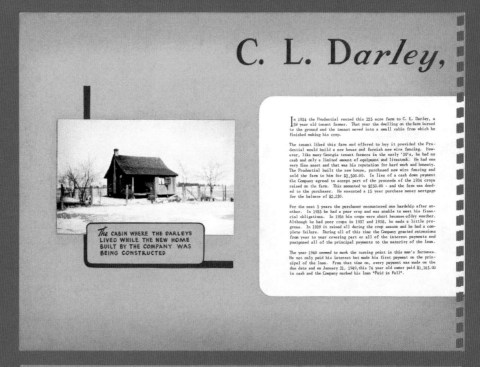

C. L. Darley,

In 1934 the Prudential rented this 225 acre farm to C. L. Darley, a 59 year old tenant farmer. That year the dwelling on the farm burned to the ground and the tenant moved into a small cabin from which he finished making his crop.

The tenant liked this farm and offered to buy it provided the Prudential would build a new house and furnish new wire fencing. However, like many Georgia tenant farmers in the early '30's, he had no cash and only a limited amount of equipment and livestock. He had one very fine asset and that was his reputation for hard work and honesty. The Prudential built the new house, purchased new wire fencing and sold the farm to him for $2,500.00. In lieu of a cash down payment the Company agreed to accept part of the proceeds of the 1934 crops raised on the farm. This amounted to $250.00 - and the farm was deeded to the purchaser. He executed a 15 year purchase money mortgage for the balance of $2,250.

For the next 5 years the purchaser encountered one hardship after another. In 1935 he had a poor crop and was unable to meet his financial obligations. In 1936 his crops were short because of dry weather. Although he had poor crops in 1937 and 1938, he made a little progress. In 1939 it rained all during the crop season and he had a complete failure. During all of this time the Company granted extensions from year to year covering part or all of the interest payments and postponed all of the principal payments to the maturity of the loan.

The year 1940 seemed to mark the turning point in this man's fortunes. He not only paid his interest but made his first payment on the principal of the loan. From that time on, every payment was made on the due date and on January 21, 1949, this 74 year old owner paid $1,185.00 in cash and the Company marked his loan "Paid in Full".

The CABIN WHERE THE DARLEYS LIVED WHILE THE NEW HOME BUILT BY THE COMPANY WAS BEING CONSTRUCTED

MITCHELL COUNTY, GEORGIA

The FARM HOUSE BUILT BY THE COMPANY IN 1934

MR. and MRS. C. L. DARLEY

Management when it acquired Merrill Lynch's relocation unit during the 1989 purchase of its real estate franchises. The ability to offer a relocation service greatly increased sales opportunities for PREA franchisees. Prudential Relocation was soon serving more than 400 corporations, and 50 percent of its volume was coming from *Fortune* 500 companies.

Seeking a New Direction for Prudential-Bache.

Throughout much of the 1980s, as Prudential struggled with finding the proper role for its new brokerage wing, the company discovered how challenging being a pioneer could be. In 1984, Prudential-Bache lost $113 million, a record for Wall Street. Prudential countered speculations that it was seeking to sell the subsidiary by making a $100 million cash contribution to its operating fund and extending it a $50 million line of credit. Prudential-Bache rebounded the next year, posting a $9 million gain on

Mario Acquista (left)
with colleague Vincenzo
Platania in Milan.
PRICOA Vita, now
Prumerica Life, introduced
the Living Needs Benefit,
convertible term life
policies, and family
income policies in Italy.

MARIO ACQUISTA

I arrived in PRICOA to work and to profit. There, I would also learn directly from experience. At the beginning of my career, mistakenly, I would impose limitations on myself. Unfortunately, one of these limitations didn't allow me to insure my cousin Luigi, who was 30 years old, had two children and a wife, and was head of a small business with big plans. Two years ago, Luigi died. There is not a value to Luigi's affections; they are priceless. But the lack of financial support that his family faces has a price.

From then on, I learned there aren't any limitations. I understood that I can't estimate how long people that I meet are going to live. I only know that I can really protect them.

Mario Acquista, Rome, Italy

revenues of $1.8 billion.

Around that same time, Prudential-Bache began to explore a new direction, toward what *The New York Times* called the "financially chic, but complex and risky business" of merchant and investment banking. Ball's "Project '89," as the venture was called, set forth an ambitious goal: to make Prudential-Bache one of the top five investment banks in the country by 1989. The subsequent 1986 buildup began with the

recruitment of 26 senior investment bankers from other firms and 29 research analysts to bolster the stock research department. Large numbers of additional (and highly compensated) investment bankers were hired in the next 18 months.

The new direction proved to be an expensive mistake. (It wasn't the first time. Paine Webber and Hutton had both tried the same tack and were forced to settle for niches. Prudential, correctly, was not interested in filling niches with its

CAROL WHITESELL

A claim form was received, and the medical portion of the form and the diagnosis were not complete. When I called the home, I spoke to the insured's mother, who was very evasive. A week later, I called back, but again, the insured wasn't home, and his mother wouldn't give me any information.

About two days after my second call, the insured called me back. He was a young man, in fact the same age that I was at the time, 29.

He said, "I'm sure my mother gave you a real hard time, and I apologize. She has a very hard time dealing with this, but I have AIDS."

The hair on my arms just stood up. He spoke for 45 minutes about how he had to get his financial affairs in order. You couldn't even comprehend what they were going through. That was just the start of many, many claims with the diagnosis of AIDS. That was a big thing going from the '70s into the '80s.

Carol Whitesell, Dresher, Pennsylvania

Prudential volunteers come out each year to lend their time and support to the St. Clare summer camp sessions run by the AIDS Resource Foundation for Children.

subsidiary.) Project '89 had required an enormous investment in recruiting specialists. Dismantling the project proved painful as well. The company was forced to let go about 400 investment bankers at the end of 1989. Project '89 also further skewed the firm's already fuzzy identity.

The foray into investment banking proved a valuable lesson for Prudential-Bache. While the restructuring caused major disruptions in 1990—including a sizable loss that year—it positioned the firm to enter the 1990s as a more strategically focused and profitable organization. And it most certainly brought the brokerage more directly under its parent's scrutiny.

The Need for a Comprehensive Strategy.
On paper, Prudential entered the 1990s feeling, as ever, extremely prosperous. In the decade spanning 1980 to 1990, Prudential's assets had more than doubled. But Prudential was far more vulnerable than it appeared. The 1980s saw a

By the 1890s, Prudential was a prosperous insurance company with thousands of employees and more than a million policyholders in 17 states. In 1892, it completed a fine, new building in Newark. This 11-story skyscraper, bearing a remarkable resemblance to the home office of British Prudential in London, exuded permanence and stability.

A Rock to Build a Reputation Upon

In addition to accommodating the demands of an ever-expanding company, the intention behind this edifice was that it was to symbolize to all policyholders—present and future—that Prudential was here to stay. But as a corporate symbol, the building for some reason didn't quite work. Author William Carr described in *From Three Cents a Week* ... how Prudential found a symbol that was

strong enough to represent the company for more than a century: "What the Prudential still needed was a symbol which would indicate its strength, its dependability. ... The Prudential Building wouldn't do; it was tried in some advertisements which called the Pru a 'Tower of Strength,' but somehow they didn't quite reach people.

"Then, in 1896, a young New York advertising man named Mortimer Remington, who was with the J. Walter Thompson agency, was introduced by his father-in-law to John F. Dryden, who suggested that Remington try to devise a service mark for the company. Remington succeeded, but the source of his inspiration is a matter of dispute. One story has it that, while riding on a train from Newark to New York, he passed Laurel Hill, a rocky elevation rising out of the Jersey Meadows, and noticed that it looked like the Rock of Gibraltar. According to another version, he came across a picture of Gibraltar in a book in the Astor Library in New York. Copying the picture, he lettered across the face of the Rock the legend: 'The Prudential Has the Strength of Gibraltar.'

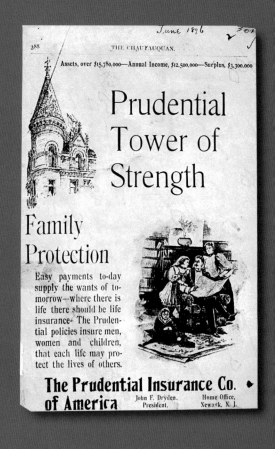

"Regardless of which version is true, one fact is certain: on August 20, 1896, *Leslie's Weekly* carried the first advertisement that showed the Rock of Gibraltar and carried the words, 'The Prudential Has the Strength of Gibraltar.'"

Remington's idea has most certainly stood the test of time. Even today, there's hardly a more recognizable symbol in America than "The Rock."

dramatic change in the economic environment as the Federal Reserve raised interest rates to combat inflation. This change strained life insurance products while making alternative investment products, such as mutual funds, far more attractive. While the company's brokerage subsidiary gave Prudential the capacity to offer these new products, Prudential remained slow in responding to changing customer needs and new technology-driven distribution systems.

Some within Prudential referred to it as "big company disease," the result of taking too much comfort in large cash reserves while failing to pay attention to increasingly rapid external changes. Others called it "mutual malaise." One consequence of this insularity was unresponsiveness to the customer, whose business it continued to take for granted. Robert Winters recently said that "overcoming the complacency of a successful organization" was a persistent

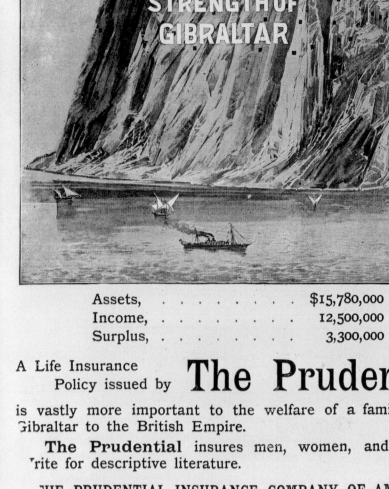

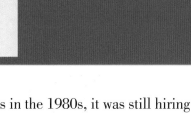

Above: Mortimer Remington,
ca. 1896.
Opposite: The short-lived ad as
it appeared in *The Chautauquan,*
June 1896.
Left: Although there have been
many incarnations of the symbol,
Mortimer Remington's idea
has endured in Prudential's
advertising.

issue during his eight years as Prudential's leader. "No one thought we needed to get any better," he said. "My greatest challenge was to help the organization understand the need to change and constantly improve."

The truth was that the company had grown huge and somewhat complacent. It had never been nimble because it had never needed to be. For example, while the company was rolling out an array of mutual funds as well as complex insurance products in the 1980s, it was still hiring and training its huge sales force—20,000 agents— in ways not demonstrably different from 1965.

Furthermore, the company's organizational structure and lack of high-level monitoring had created a substantial control issue. Addressing this period in Prudential's history, a February 1997 *New York Times* article remarked, "The company had already expanded beyond [life insurance], but instead of operating under a

One hundred Prudential employees served in Operations Desert Shield and Desert Storm in 1990 and 1991. Proud of the sacrifices of its employees, the company ran congratulatory ads in each employee's local newspaper and hosted parties across the nation for its returning heroes.

PATRICIA BRZOZOWSKI

I joined Prudential in March 1989 and had been there for just over a year when I was activated to go to Desert Storm.

My activation meant that my salary was going to drop because the Air Force paid less than Prudential, and I had just bought a house. My management team was instrumental in getting Prudential to make up the difference in salaries.

While I was away, Prudential people kept in touch to keep my spirits up. When I got back, Prudential gave each division that had a reservist $1,000 to throw a party to say thank you to the division for everything they did. They also put a nice advertisement in the newspaper saying, "Prudential Salutes our Returning Reservists."

If Prudential hadn't made up the difference in my salary, I would not have been able to make my house and car payments. That was a defining moment in my career with Prudential.

Patricia Brzozowski, Jacksonville, Florida

comprehensive strategy, those businesses, as well as the five regional headquarters of the life insurance division, addressed the world on their own terms. ... Each of the units had its own computer system, its own purchasing system and its own advertising program. They did not share information about their customers, so the company could make the most of each relationship, and all too often one Prudential unit would be elbowing another for the same piece of business." In

addition, a rigid chain of command hampered flexibility and discouraged the kind of cross-fertilization the company needed to develop new products as well as marketing and sales strategies.

A Dark Cloud at Securities. Prudential had always been a patient—perhaps even permissive—parent. But what the parent couldn't tolerate was even the suggestion of impropriety. So, when in the winter of 1991, *Business Week* published an exposé describing how Prudential-

Bache had misled clients by selling them investments in high-risk limited partnerships, Prudential decided that something had to change.

Prudential-Bache's chairman left on Valentine's Day 1991 with no permanent replacement in sight. Bob Beck returned to oversee operations while Prudential thwarted suggestions that its subsidiary was up for sale. On April 24, Prudential-Bache announced that a new CEO would take over leadership of

the company on May 1. "May Day" would turn out to be an omen.

Before the CEO came on board, Prudential provided him with information on the firm. It briefly mentioned a potential $20 million to $30 million localized limited-partnership problem. The firm was in for a surprise, for what everyone sincerely thought to be a "localized" and (for a company with Prudential's wealth) inexpensive problem swelled into a massive embarrassment

FRED SCHUBERT

Back in the 1950s, I was working in Waco, Texas. One afternoon it was real quiet outside and then, all of a sudden, a torrential rain came. We were on the sixth floor of the Liberty Building, which is in the 900 block of Washington Avenue in Waco. The rain was splattering against the windowpanes. Then, hailstones getting bigger and bigger were hitting the windowpanes. All of a sudden, everything just turned pitch black. Then, the silence ended and it sounded like 10,000 diesel locomotives all growling at the same time. I had never heard anything like it before. The building started shaking and rocking back and forth. One of the women I worked with came up and asked me what we should do. Then, the lights went off because the electricity was blown away in the whole city. We hugged each other for what seemed like an eternity but was really only five or six minutes while all the destruction was going on outside. That's the only time I've ever hugged an office lady in my life, and I hope that my excuse was a good one!

Fred Schubert, Houston, Texas

that ultimately cost the company nearly $2 billion.

Prudential-Bache took a battering from both government regulators and the media. As one Prudential Securities executive described it, "There was more bad news every day." And "every day" lasted for two years. The good news was that favorable market conditions allowed the subsidiary to make money from 1991 to 1993. The bad news? It was under federal scrutiny the entire period.

Two things allowed Prudential-Bache, renamed Prudential Securities in 1990, to survive. The first was Prudential's determination to cooperate with investigators and assure regulators that problems had been fixed and remedies were forthcoming. But the greatest contributor to the firm's salvation was the company itself. No other brokerage could have survived the morass of legal and public scrutiny, not to mention the monetary penalties.

Throughout the ordeal, the company struggled

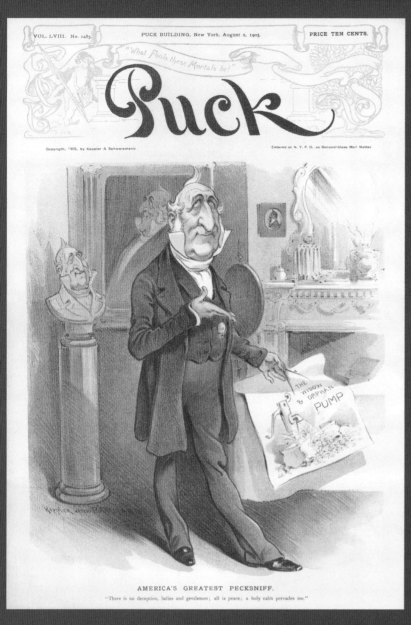

VOL. LVIII. No. 1483.   PUCK BUILDING, New York, August 2, 1905.   PRICE TEN CENTS.

"What Fools these Mortals be!"

Puck

Copyright, 1905, by Keppler & Schwarzmann   Entered at N. Y. P. O. as Second-class Mail Matter

AMERICA'S GREATEST PECKSNIFF.

"There is no deception, ladies and gentlemen; all is peace; a holy calm pervades me."

Negative perceptions of insurance companies
and agents persisted until the sweeping
reforms of New York's Armstrong
investigation, which concluded in 1906.

This excerpt from Frederick Hoffman's 1900 *History of the Prudential* shows what John Dryden was up against when he started selling industrial insurance: "Thus, in the year 1853, *The New York Times*, in a lengthy argument, maintained the view that 'He who insures his life or health must be indeed a victim of his own folly or others' knavery' and a Mr. A.B. Johnson, a Baltimore banker and writer on economic subjects, expressed

A Victim of His Own Folly

himself forcibly against the theory of life insurance and in favor of the theory and practice of savings banks, holding that all life insurance was wrong in principle and false in practice. ... It may not be out of place to give some space to Mr. Johnson's views: 'If no life insurance would provide for our families after our decease, no health insurance or club would provide for ourselves during disease, and bury us decently when dead, we should provide for these purposes for self-denying accumulations. ... Life insurance is unfavorable to domestic purity. ... In England, mothers have been convicted of murdering their infants to obtain some petty sums which certain clubs bestow for funeral expenses on members whose children die.'"

to raise morale, which the departure of half of Prudential Securities' key people had severely tested. In 1994, the firm paid off an almost $2 billion settlement, but after a three-year loss of momentum, it started to develop more cross-unit strategy. In 1994, although not yet fully recovered, Prudential Securities was the nation's fourth-largest retail brokerage firm with 6,300 brokers. In addition, first-quarter sales of $8 billion made it the 10th-largest underwriter of securities worldwide.

Walloped by Hurricane Andrew. One of the units that addressed the world on its own terms was PRUPAC, the company's property and casualty unit. The most painful consequences of the insularity described previously and the lack of oversight that came with it were brought to bear upon the company most demonstrably when Hurricane Andrew struck southern Florida in August 1992.

MARY O'MALLEY

A few weeks after Hurricane Andrew occurred, we sent down a bunch of really courageous volunteers to help those insured by Prudential as well as other people in the community. Most of the families who were most severely in need were still severely in need.

We asked Prudential people to adopt a family down in southern Florida, and they responded in such a magnificent way. In fact, Prudential people adopted over 500 of the neediest families, who were living in unbelievably terrible conditions. Most of the families still didn't have homes and were living in trailers. Some were suffering from skin cancer because they'd been continuously exposed to the sun. Others had mold on all their clothes because they had no roofs.

I went down to Florida with an 18-wheeler full of household goods and more than $20,000 in cash. Prudential people responded quickly, and they continued to respond for months afterwards.

Mary O'Malley, Newark, New Jersey

Essentially, PRUPAC was created in 1971 to provide additional products for agents whose bread and butter remained life insurance. Few expected the subsidiary to make money, and following a solid start-up, it didn't. After Dave Sherwood created the unit, PRUPAC's leadership rotated frequently and was seldom if ever piloted by anyone with property and casualty expertise.

Consistency, accountability and risk control did not receive consistent attention. PRUPAC had done the customary "probable maximum loss" calculations for Florida as a whole but had neglected to slice the pie more thinly. Meanwhile, partially because Prudential had a successful district agency in southern Florida selling lots of property and casualty, the company had accumulated a huge exposure in the area—the epicenter of Andrew's wrath.

The hurricane devastated southern Florida and nearly ruined PRUPAC as well. As one

executive put it, "We lost $1.4 billion in one afternoon."

Despite the huge financial losses, Prudential showed its true character during the crisis. The company responded with extraordinary attention to its customers. One of the first senior executives called to the scene called the region "a war zone," but within a short time, hundreds of employees from all over the country were deployed and began to serve for weeks and, in some cases,

months in the area, getting people housed, fed and back on their feet. While the company had great reasons to worry about its own well-being, those considerations took a back seat to what Prudential had been created to do: Serve those in need.

The extraordinary financial losses from Andrew could have been looked upon as a one-time stroke of bad luck. (After all, had the storm struck 20 miles farther north, Allstate would have

The Toll of the Influenza Epidemic

As World War I raged, another hardship was plaguing the world: influenza. William Carr reported in *From Three Cents a Week* ... that, in some ways, it hit Prudential even harder than the combat:

"[In 1918,] the terrible influenza epidemic was sweeping North America, having ravaged Europe. Some idea of the impact of the epidemic can be gained from these facts: in 1917, there were 51 flu deaths in Boston; by October 1, 1918, there were 202 deaths a day in that city. ... One out of four persons in the

U.S. and Canada fell ill; of every 1,000 stricken, 19 died. The total number of deaths was estimated officially at between 400,000 and 500,000. ...

"For the people of Prudential, it was the most demanding time they had ever known as a group. Although Newark was not hit as badly as most cities—the death rate went up only 250 percent there—the Home Office, where claims had to be processed, was undermanned because of the number of clerks who were sick. And in the agency offices across the continent men and women worked valiantly to serve their policyholders in a time of heightened need.

"From September 26 to October 19, 1918, the Pru paid $1,000,000 in influenza death claims. In one day it paid $506,000 in all kinds of death claims, a record up to that time.

"One of the hardest hit cities was Philadelphia, where the death rate shot up 700 percent. Harry I. Leonard ... found the epidemic 'unbelievable.' ... Undertakers could not handle so many funerals. The district ran out of coffins. At the office he worked out of, Philadelphia No. 9, everybody pitched in to help adjust and pay claims as fast as possible, but even so, long lines formed at the cashier's window as though seeking tickets for a Broadway hit.

"One day Leonard's boss, R.J. Pedrick, realized that the agent had been working for weeks in houses visited by the deadly flu.

"'What do you do for medication, Harry?' he asked.

"'My prescription calls for a quart a day,' Leonard replied, 'but I believe I'm a little ahead of the prescription.'"

Left: A nurse treats an ill employee in the company's Infirmary. Prudential established the Infirmary in the North Building in 1911 to care for the legion of home office workers.
Opposite: The emergency hospital at Camp Funston, Fort Riley, Kansas, in 1918, site of the first reported case of the century's deadliest influenza outbreak. The calamitous epidemic claimed approximately 21.7 million victims worldwide—more people than were wounded in all of World War I.

---

been the greater financial victim.) However, the organizational and oversight habits that had made Hurricane Andrew so costly were causing even more serious problems across the Hudson at Prudential Securities.

Facing the Music. While the problems at PRUPAC and Prudential Securities could be looked upon as isolated, unforeseeable events, the continuing absence of growth in Prudential's core life insurance business could not. As *The New York Times* reported, "Prudential's central problem stems from the fact that life insurance— while still the largest single part of the company's business—has been steadily losing appeal to Americans far more interested in investing in the booming stock market for a more comfortable retirement than in planning for death."

Through the first nine months of 1994, overall performance dropped dramatically from the same period the previous year. Life insurance sales

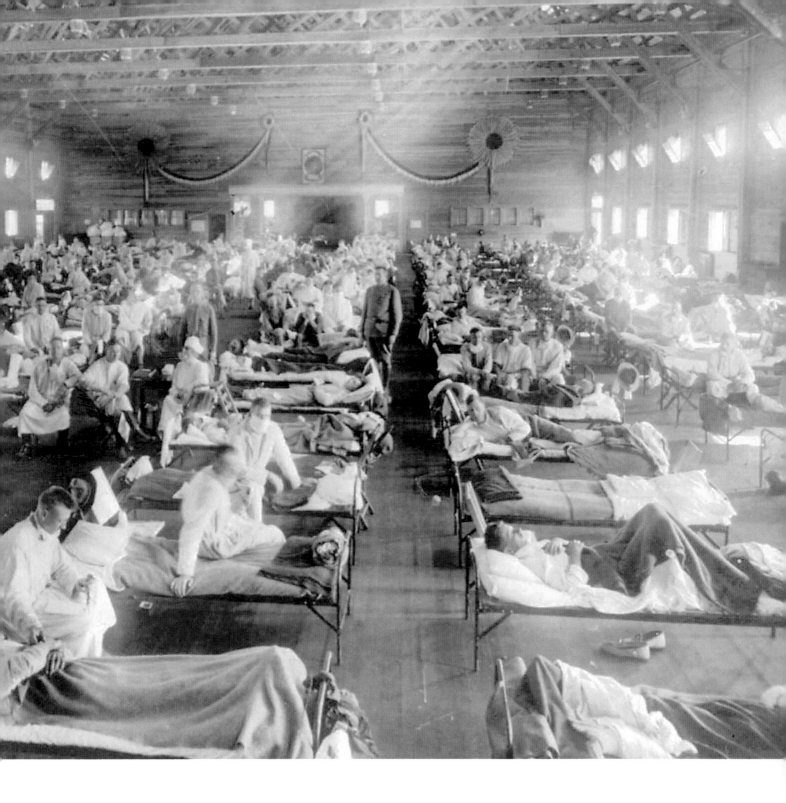

were down 16 percent from the same period in 1993. Contributing to the reduction was the loss of more than 2,000 agents from January through the end of September. (Between 1990 and 1994, the number of agents dropped from roughly 20,000 to 14,000.)

Prudential International Insurance remained strong. The unit's $427 million in new business sales was well ahead of plan. The increase was spurred by Prudential of Japan, which posted $15 million in

earnings in the third quarter alone, 30 percent of its full-year projection.

While the company was aware of the confluence of forces pressing upon it— competition and market pressure, the changing needs of the consumer—it seemed unable to react quickly and decisively enough. Prudential reported 1994 losses of $907 million as its capital base was reduced by $1.2 billion, to $9.5 billion, largely due to charges taken related to Prudential

Above: The role of the Life Planner goes beyond meetings and signatures. Life Planner Yushi Murakami of the Hiroshima Agency meets with policyholders Mr. and Mrs. Kikkawa.

Opposite: Prudential began testing the concept of the Life Planner system in the Japanese market more than 20 years ago. Since its incorporation in 1987, Prudential of Japan has led the nation in changing the face of its life insurance.

NAOKO WATANABE

I am a seventh-grader at the Bunkyo Girls School, and my father Ichiro Watanabe works at Prudential. He has always been someone who puts his heart into everything: baseball, skating, boxing, ping-pong, golf and prize goldfish-keeping. He always has a purpose, and so he is successful. He has attended Prudential conventions eight times and has brought me along seven times with my mother and younger sister.

Last year, he became the sales manager. No matter how late he comes home, he is up by 6 in the morning and always has a few words for me and my younger sister.

He has also always talked in his sleep. When he was a life planner and selling insurance, he would say things in his sleep like "Thank you," "I understand what you are saying," etc. Once he became the sales manager, he would talk in a loud voice, saying, "You can if you really try," "Close," etc.

My father is at work even in his dreams. He must truly love his work.

Naoko Watanabe, Funabashi City, Japan

Securities sales of limited partnerships. But the operating figures alone were enough to provoke the company to seek a remedy. Vice Chairman Garnett Keith stated, "Our nine-month results for 1994 were not a happy story. ... We needed to make serious and immediate adjustments to our operations." And serious they were, probably the most serious and extensive in the history of the company. Prudential reduced staff and overhead, but that was only a quick fix.

Further complicating matters was the impending change in the top leadership. CEO Bob Winters, who had been with Prudential for 41 years, had told the board in 1987 that he would retire before he was 63, and he indeed announced his intention to retire in 1994. In determining Winters' successor, the board made a bold decision. On October 20, 1994, Prudential announced that Arthur F. Ryan, at the time second-in-command at Chase Manhattan

Corporation, would become the new CEO and chairman of the company. For the first time in the company's history, the new CEO would come not only from outside the company but also from outside the insurance industry altogether.

Serious Challenges for New Leadership.

Ryan's background in the highly competitive world of Wall Street had taught him that the problems facing Prudential didn't mysteriously happen. They resulted, rather, from paying insufficient attention to the outside pressures and market functions that define mainstream business. To counter this inattention, Ryan quickly imposed on Prudential an increased sense of accountability and consequence—both internal and external—and began examining each subsidiary as if Prudential were a public company. Additionally, Prudential had to learn to redouble its efforts to focus on something outside the firm: the customer.

VICTOR HOWARD

As a part of the Operations and Systems MDP (Management Development Program), I was assigned to the Credit Control and Margin Loan area at Prudential Securities in New York. During my time there, Art Ryan and Bob Golden, along with other senior executives, were meeting in our building. As a part of the meeting, Art Ryan and Bob Golden toured several areas within the building, and I heard that they were going to make a stop in our area. When they came into our area, they went into my manager's office. I thought to myself that this was my break and that I should go over and introduce myself. However, I didn't, and the group of executives left the area. I began kicking myself because I knew that I had missed a prime opportunity to make a good first impression and meet some very powerful men within the company.

Well, later that day, I was on my way to meet my executive sponsor (Joseph Luino) when the group of executives stepped out into the hall. Joseph introduced me to them and further explained that I was working in his area

Prudential's reluctance to change was further exacerbated by the company's limited understanding—after three decades of diversi-fication—of what it had become: not just an insurance company with subsidiaries, but a large and potentially powerful financial services company.

The new CEO faced the difficult challenge of simultaneously improving both short- and long-term circumstances—stop the bleeding while also heightening Prudential's competitiveness within the financial services arena. But Ryan's efforts would quickly hit a serious roadblock and present challenges to his leadership that were far more extensive than any he had imagined when he took on the job.

The "Sales Practices Issues." Ryan had been at Prudential just a few months when, in early 1995, the company was hit by a series of lawsuits and regulatory investigations based on claims that the company had for many years been

*as a part of my Module 1 assignment with the MDP. We
began a brief conversation about how things were going and
they let me know that they were available if I ever wanted to
talk further. This meeting meant a lot to me not because of
the fact of who they were but that they actually took time
to talk to me. The executives showed interest in what I was
doing and made themselves available in the future.*

Victor Howard, Jacksonville, Florida

In 1981, Prudential
introduced financial
services to its 50 million
customers through
Prudential-Bache
Securities.

mis-selling its individual life insurance products. Among the most common claims made were that policies were sold with misleading promises that dividends and other policy values would be sufficient to cover some or all of the cost of the new policies.

These accusations, referred to internally as the "sales practices issues," sent the company into a tailspin. Although scores of companies during this period were hit with similar suits,

Prudential garnered most of the regulatory and media attention. Moreover, this was Prudential, and life insurance was its soul.

To let the matter consume the company would have been fatal. Ryan had to find the means to resolve the issue while continuing to move the company forward. If the claims were legitimate, he had to address them. At the same time, as steward for all the company's policyowners, he had to assure them that company funds would

The former PRUPAC office in Scottsdale, Arizona.

A t one point, I transferred from Prudential Property and Casualty in Holmdel to Western Operations–Scottsdale. I was fairly new, so I was wearing white shirts, ties and suits. The Scottsdale people dressed more casually.

At one point, an irate insured who we decided not to renew started making terroristic threats against the under-writer. He wanted to know the underwriter's name, and the nervous customer service rep said that I was the underwriter.

He continued to call and one time actually said that he was flying to Arizona from Riverside, California, and that he was going to kill Joe Ritchie. So Lew Bolitho called Scottsdale police, who called Riverside police, and they found out that he was flying to Arizona.

The day he was flying in, unbeknownst to me, everybody dressed up like me—both women and men wore suits, white shirts, ties. And all the nametags on the desks had Joe Ritchie on them. They figured if the guy walked in, he wouldn't know who Joe Ritchie was.

Joe Ritchie, Holmdel, New Jersey

only be expended under appropriate circumstances.

Company representatives quickly went on record, stating that the practices alleged in the lawsuits were "unacceptable and against company policy." Nevertheless, under Ryan's direction, the company examined the claims and its own practices and controls during the time period in question (the 1980s and early 1990s). The company ultimately concluded that there had been a sales practices problem and that it required a comprehensive company response.

The sales practices matter was, above all else, a test of character and integrity. Ryan has often been described as a man who explains business decisions by saying, "It's the right thing to do." In this case, it turned out that the right thing to do—for Prudential and its customers—was to admit wrongdoing, to take steps to assure it would not happen again, and to make good with every customer with a valid sales practices complaint.

YVONNE YAMATANI

I'm a senior underwriting case manager. For the most part, I really love this Client Acquisition Process. We now talk to clients over the phone, and some of the conversations can be very interesting.

I had the opportunity to speak to a 67-year-old male about a year or so ago. Going through the risk questions, we came to that ever-famous "Have you ever been treated or diagnosed with AIDS, any AIDS-related condition or any sexually transmitted diseases?" He paused, and then I heard, "Young lady, I'm 67 years old, and it's been years since I've transmitted anything."

Yvonne Yamatani, Dresher, Pennsylvania

In the Client Acquisition Process, representatives take an active part in getting to know clients and their needs.

That is precisely what Ryan promised to do.

Keeping that promise to remedy all legitimate sales practices claims was a massive challenge. Members of the company's senior executive team were charged with negotiating and implementing a settlement strategy with regulators. They also faced the task of ensuring that the resulting agreements would allow Prudential to move forward as a financially viable institution. The regulators' Multi-State Task Force issued its formal report in July 1996. In accepting that report, Prudential committed to instituting a remediation program for sales practices complainants, which included substantial remedies for legitimate claims. The Task Force also recommended and the company agreed to pay a series of fines to the states. Ultimately, the remediation program described in the Task Force report was enhanced in the context of settlements with several additional states and in connection

In 1964, *Fortune* magazine wrote a piece on the extraordinary growth and influence of Prudential. The article focused on a factor too often underappreciated in the insurance business: the sales agent. "It is not, after all, the Shankses and the Beals who have made Prudential what it is," *Fortune* said. "Those billions in premiums have to be sweated out of the consciences of the people in what is still the most agonizing person-to-person sales duel on the American scene. The root strength of any life insurance company lies in its agency force."

Above and Beyond

Confirming this notion, author William Carr recounts some tales of Prudential agents going above and beyond to make a sale in his book *From Three Cents a Week* ...:

"Given the tensions and the pressures, the self-doubts and the need to find inner resources of strength, it is inevitable that agents should often find themselves taking advantage of all manner of circumstances to close a sale. In Sioux Falls a special agent, Earl Snyder, waited on customers to help

with the settlement of the principal class action lawsuit based on the same issues. Federal Judge Alfred M. Wolin approved the final terms of the settlement as fair, under which Prudential would eventually provide remedies to sales practices claimants that cost approximately $2.6 billion.

The remediation program is virtually complete. As it wound down, Judge Wolin commented that the program was "an extraordinary success" and commended Prudential

for keeping true to its promise to fairly remedy all legitimate sales practices claims, all of which was achieved while maintaining and enhancing the company's overall financial condition.

We Will Make Prudential a Winner Again. The wrenching self-examination exacted by the sales practices ordeal became the springboard for changes long overdue at Prudential. After the settlement, Ryan stated in an interview, "The settlement offers us the opportunity to direct our

out a drive-in restaurant owner who was suddenly overwhelmed with business, then sold him a policy on his 15-year-old son. When a young man drove his car into the automobile of Wayne Tooman, a special agent in Muscatine, Iowa, Tooman used the encounter to open a series of conversations which ended with his selling a $10,000 policy on the other driver's life and health insurance coverage on his mother. Cy Seltman, a special agent in Pittsburgh, having failed to persuade a prospect, was leaving when he slipped on the ice; 'It wouldn't make any difference if I were hurt,' he called out to the client, 'because I've got the kind of insurance you should have' — and the householder finally gave in and bought the policy Seltman had recommended. As a tornado wrecked

much of Fargo, North Dakota, special agent Calvin J. Dargan, huddling in a basement with a young couple and their baby, got their signature on a health insurance policy; at that moment, all the young husband wanted to know was, 'Where do I sign?' In Oklahoma, an agent even sold a policy to a policeman who had stopped him for speeding."

Above: Jacksonville agents gather in 1954 to discuss sales strategy.
Left: Director of Agencies Stan Gagner and DAAD's Linda Christian proudly show off the sales figures reached by the North Central Home Office's district agents in 1968.

energy and focus on the challenges at hand— continuing to place our customers first and improving our performance." Prudential would proceed to examine everything: who it was and how it thought, planned and did business.

The experience helped unify the company and, more importantly, dissolve the insular and independent cultures that had emerged within it. The fact that Prudential began—perhaps for the first time in decades—to do business with a

single vision aided the changes immensely.

Ryan had to make clear to everyone at every level of the company just what Prudential was— and in fact had been—for some time, not just a seller of life insurance but a leader in providing for growth and protection of clients' assets. Within that model, the company could then identify and develop new platforms for growth. As a February 1997 *New York Times* article reported, "No longer, [Ryan] decreed, was Prudential to be first

I n the mid-1980s, Prudential's Canadian Operations was led by Ron Barbaro, a former insurance agent who was involved in many charitable activities around Toronto, including an AIDS hospice and treatment center. While touring the facility, Ron met a seriously ill young man, who identified himself as a Prudential policyholder. He told Ron he wanted to see his parents one more time, but he had no money for the trip, although he owned a $20,000 life insurance policy. Touched by his story, Ron asked how he could help. The young man said, "Help me die with dignity."

Ron was so moved by the request that he met with his actuarial, claims, medical and legal staff and asked that they find a way to satisfy the young man's request quickly.

In 1988, Prudential's Canadian Operation quietly introduced an accelerated death benefit option. At no additional cost, Prudential gave its terminally ill Canadian policyholders access to the proceeds of their life insurance while they were still alive to help pay for medical care, family needs or anything else they wanted.

Opposite: Agent Linda Roberts (right) talks with Jan Anderson, whose family was the first beneficiary of the Living Needs Benefit in the United States. Over 1,500 customers across the world used policy funds to obtain organ transplants, establish care in nursing homes and to ease the burdens of terminal illnesses.

and foremost a life insurance company. … He had been watching the revolution that had … transformed banks into financial powerhouses again, while seemingly leaving life insurance as something your father recalled with nostalgia." Money management and financial services would, from the mid-1990s on, take equal importance with insurance.

This refocusing of priorities demanded a swift reassembly of Prudential's upper-level management.

New leaders were brought in to address Prudential's traditional weaknesses in risk management, marketing, human resources, and technical and processing services. Ryan retained executives in areas in which the company excelled. Within two years of Ryan's arrival, 12 of the 14 executives who reported directly to him were new to their posts. Of the top 150 executives, two-thirds were new, about half recruited from outside Prudential. As *The Wall Street Journal*

Prompted by news of the Canadian program, politicians and regulators asked if we would develop a similar benefit for U.S. policyholders, and many offered to help expedite the regulatory process.

In 1990, Prudential introduced the Living Needs Benefit rider in the United States. This rider expanded on the Canadian benefit, providing for accelerated death benefit payments for the terminally ill, those in need of life-saving organ transplants and those permanently confined to nursing homes. Because the benefit was made available "at cost," it was available to existing customers as well as new life insurance purchasers.

As a direct result of Prudential's efforts, accelerated death benefit options are now a common feature of U.S. life insurance products. A similar option has been developed for our Group Life customers. Over $110 million has been paid out by Prudential in accelerated death benefits, aiding roughly 1,500 customers and their families.

Marty Berkowitz, Newark, New Jersey

described it, the addition of "battle-tested" people from outside made "once-insular Prudential ... something of a United Nations of the financial-services world."

In November 1995, Prudential announced a major reorganization designed not only to reduce costs but also, for the first time, to elevate product and money management to the same importance as distribution. The conversion of the remaining five regional headquarters into customer service operations resulted in further streamlining.

Fitting the Company to the New Mission. With Prudential's new focus as a "provider of life insurance and investment products," each business unit was scrutinized to ensure appropriate fit and market viability. Beginning in early 1995, Prudential sold its home mortgage business, its Canadian life insurance branch and its reinsurance organization. Unprofitable units of Prudential's health care

MACK GARRETT

Even as Prudential grew by leaps and bounds, it maintained its support of small businesses by providing a variety of flexible plans that met their special needs.

I guess two of the first clients I had were a man and wife who owned a small business here in Atlanta. They had done no estate planning at all. He was a very bad diabetic, and when we tried to get life insurance on him, they rated him an "H."

But we were able to get some group insurance through Prudential's GSP. It was a small group health insurance program that also offered life insurance. While he was on a dialysis machine, I visited him to finish the estate work, and he said to me, "You know, if it weren't for my family, I wouldn't do this. But I'm doing it strictly for them." He died not long after.

Through the estate planning and through Prudential, we were able to save that family an estate that's now worth well over $3 million or $4 million. The young sons were able to continue the business. They said, "Thank God you came along when you did." That's the sort of thing that really makes you feel good about what you do.

Mack Garrett, Atlanta, Georgia

operation were also sold, and the remainder were consolidated. In 1996, executives overhauled the company's real estate investments, selling most of its $5.6 billion of office buildings, hotels and other properties.

Both the new organizational structure and the new faces populating Prudential reflected the kind of customer-focused strategic thinking the company badly needed. Greater attention to customer needs and buying habits resulted in the creation of new products. In 1997, a number of previously independent investment units were gathered under the umbrella of Prudential Investments, which soon created several successful new mutual funds and annuities.

Additionally, the group life division separated from Prudential HealthCare in 1997 and began operating as a stand-alone business. Its new focus and aggressive growth strategy paid off as the unit posted $122 million in new sales in 1997, more

than double the prior year's total.

Prudential's new strategy and vision also made money management an increasingly significant part of the company's identity throughout the 1990s. Historically, asset management at Prudential had been a support function, and a quarter-century ago, roughly 90 to 95 percent of Prudential's money under management was from its general insurance account. By the late 1990s, however, more than 60 percent of the money Prudential managed came from mutual funds and institutional clients.

Marketing at Prudential also got an overhaul. To begin with, Prudential enjoyed enormous brand recognition, but the public thought of it almost exclusively as an insurance company. Second, Prudential's advertising and other marketing programs were spread among a variety of outside agencies. The resulting lack of consistency and coherence contributed to the

Thom Powers' grandparents Len Lesnik and Evelyn Bugayski Lesnik celebrate Evelyn's 20th anniversary with Prudential in 1966. Evelyn started her career with Prudential when she left high school; Len began work with the Prudential in 1926, interrupting his career for four years while he served in the Navy in WWII. Both worked at the Mid-America Home Office in Chicago.

THOM POWERS

My family's history with Prudential dates back to the turn of the century. I had two great-great-great-uncles who worked for Prudential until 1906. My grandfather had 48 years with Prudential. He retired in 1972 but is still very active with fellow Prudential retirees in Florida. Bruno Pinkos tells a story about the fire at Our Lady of the Angels School in Chicago. Dozens of people died. My grandfather was in charge of the claims at the time. Bruno remembers how my grandfather grabbed the checkbook and ran outside, where he started handing Bruno checks to pass out on Michigan Avenue.

My grandmother also worked for Prudential as well as my great-great-uncle, who was an agent for 40 years. I have been with Prudential for six years. The combined years of service among all the generations of my family equals about 250 years.

Thom Powers, Englewood, Colorado

company's skewed public image. To achieve a more consistent identity and message, the company assembled an in-house advertising staff and terminated its associations with outside agencies. Third, Prudential began to bring this consistency to the company's global marketing and public relations.

Given the roller coaster ride of Ryan's first two years—and the long-term strategic and structural changes introduced during this period—what

surprised many was that Prudential's renewed customer focus produced an unexpectedly quick turnaround in the bottom line. Between 1996 and 1997, earnings, before charges for sales practices and income taxes, increased 50 percent. Also in 1996, the company converted its bookkeeping to generally accepted accounting procedures and was now monitoring its results on the same basis as most of corporate America. Perhaps most importantly, 1997 saw Prudential begin to pick up

Frederick L. Hoffman

Throughout its history, Prudential has been populated by characters; however, many couldn't match the colorfulness of Frederick Hoffman, as William Carr wrote in his book *From Three Cents a Week ...* : "Another figure of some consequence in the Prudential [during the early 1900s] was Dr. Frederick L. Hoffman, who came to America from Germany at the age of nineteen and eventually became the Pru's chief statistician and a vice president. In every generation of the Pru there seems to have been at least one especially colorful person, and Hoffman filled that role during his 41 years with the company. He was witty, daring, insatiably curious, unorthodox, and high-spirited—sometimes to the annoyance of his more staid colleagues.

"At one party, for example, a woman went up to Hoffman and said, 'I've often wondered, Doctor — what is the difference between a statistician and an actuary?' 'About $25,000 a year, my dear,' Hoffman replied. Most of those present laughed at the joke, but not all. When Louis R. Menagh, an actuary who later became president of the Pru, was 80 years old, he still remembered the incident with anger, although it had occurred more than 35 years earlier.

"During his long career with the Pru, Hoffman traveled all over the world, investigating the facts of life and death. From one of his trips, in 1901, he brought back what he called 'a Chip' of the Rock of Gibraltar—a 2,000-pound block of stone. Because of his concern for the victims of disease, Hoffman played a significant part in the founding of the American Cancer Society and the National Tuberculosis Association. During the 1920s, when flying was still regarded as extremely hazardous, he traveled by air frequently. His publications fill a considerable length of shelf in the Prudential's museum. ... Hoffman's statistical bureau was considered the best in the Western Hemisphere."

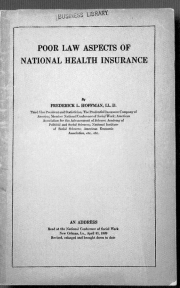

Top: Dr. Hoffman, ca. 1910. A 1927 article in the *Newark Sunday Call* said of the doctor, "He is small, wiry and nervous; cares nothing whatever for the conventions of society, and this because his mind is entirely saturated with other things. ... He can tell you Ty Cobb's record for 1914 and he can tell you how many died of the pip in Samoa in 1643."

Above: Transcript from an address given by Dr. Hoffman at the National Conference of Social Work in New Orleans, April 1920.

---

market share for the first time in several years with many of its key products, including mutual funds, annuities and securities. The following year saw an even more dramatic improvement.

Technology Serving the Customer. Having eliminated or streamlined some of Prudential's more unwieldy business units, the next step was to excel in those that remained. To be truly competitive again, the company had to do two things: listen carefully to its customers and invest in technology to serve them better.

The company's more comprehensive identity demanded that it embrace technology as a means to respond to changing consumer habits and the evolving marketing and distribution strategies of its increasing number of competitors. So in 1995, Ryan brought in new leadership to spearhead Prudential's business-wide technological overhaul.

For the first time, Prudential began benchmarking technological performance,

*W*hen *I first started in the business, a customer was someone who dealt with you maybe because his father or family had dealt with you.*

They depended on their stock broker for everything. Maybe they got The Wall Street Journal, *and they did a little reading, but primarily they depended on that broker to tell them what to do with their money. Now, we have e-trade. We have CNBC. We have* Money *magazine.*

People are better informed so it makes us more responsible for our advice. We really have to be on top of things and very well-trained. We have to be aware of the customers' needs and what they are looking for to make sure that we do the right thing for the customer.

Terry Brehony, Bala Cynwyd, Pennsylvania

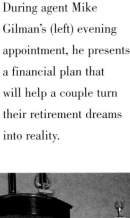

During agent Mike Gilman's (left) evening appointment, he presents a financial plan that will help a couple turn their retirement dreams into reality.

measuring it not against internal progress or other insurance companies—but against outside financial services firms. Only such measures would make Prudential what it wanted to be: a leader in financial services technology. As Prudential's chief information officer stated, "It is essential that Prudential become more 21st century and less 19th century. Technology can do that." In response, Prudential would devote more than $2 billion to new technology in the late '90s —more than $1 billion in 1998 alone.

The mid-1990s would see the emergence of an even trickier technological conundrum: The World Wide Web was going mainstream. Nothing about the company would remain untouched. The Internet would become a distribution issue, a venue for widespread promotion of Prudential's identity and image, and a catalyst for reconceiving business processes related to asset and money management. Neither Ryan nor his

GAIL CRAWFORD

*W*hen I first arrived at Prudential 27 years ago, I had no idea that I would make Prudential a career choice. That changed when I met Prudential's Constance O. Garretson, who was the first Black woman to become a Chartered Life Underwriter. She and other women of color like her became my role models for life. They also introduced me to an organization called the Minority Interchange (MI), Inc. MI gave me new knowledge, a network of new friends and a new career. But most importantly, it gave me the confidence and the leadership skills that I have successfully honed over the years.

As an employee of Prudential, I have seen many changes. The biggest change has been the way in which the company has embraced diversity. In the year 2000, I was recognized as a "Champion of Diversity," which is a Prudential award given to employees who exhibit extraordinary leadership in the area of diversity. My work as a leader of diversity is my dream job. What I see in my work makes me proud of Prudential, my management and my team.

Gail Crawford, Newark, New Jersey

Constance Garretson during a 1974 PICAA trip to Bangkok, Thailand. Garretson served Prudential for 30 years and acted as founding Secretary for the Prudential Foundation.

lieutenants were ignorant of the rapidly emerging online business world, but they also knew that they were leading a company encumbered by deeply entrenched and, in some cases, outmoded business models. Prudential still had some serious catching up to do.

One Prudential. Much of the new technology brought into Prudential in the mid- and late 1990s was designed to serve the company's keystone initiative, "One Prudential." Conceptually,

One Prudential operated and continues to operate on two fronts: first, structuring the company and all of its subsidiaries to think and plan as a single entity, and, second, conveying this identity to the public and taking the fullest advantage of Prudential's phenomenal 96 percent brand recognition.

Describing the concept was simple. However, the execution of that concept was and continues to be complex. Although One Prudential was introduced in 1996, the nature of the initiative

ensures that it is a work in progress, even as Prudential enters a new century. The reasons are twofold: One Prudential requires new and highly sophisticated training mechanisms as well as massive technological integration.

On the retail side of One Prudential, the new initiative meant developing cross-selling strategies and benchmarking sales performance. In the past, the company had measured its sales performance solely against its previous year's statistics. Performance henceforth would be measured against the higher and more objective standards of the industry at large. Raising the bar quickly increased agent productivity by 30 percent. Such heightened performance and aggressive cross-selling strategies can only be sustained, however, by instilling the One Prudential concept in the company's front-line sales units.

While One Prudential has changed how the

LOUISE COOK

Technology has changed so quickly.

When I first started, I did the agent's comp on punch cards. You typed in information, and the machine punched holes. Then you merged all the cards behind the agent's main card, using sorters and collators. Everything was then processed through what was called the tab machine, which totaled everything and created a statement. Then the checks were typed up.

The first mainframe filled at least half a room, and it was 16K. You didn't have disk space per se. Data was contained on big platters that you carried. One of the tech people we had then fixed everything with a hammer. He'd bang away and had a great time. Now we're issuing laptops, and agents are using top-of-the-line Thinkpads.

Louise Cook, Minneapolis, Minnesota

Above: In 1926, a punch card system was introduced to Prudential for mortgage loan accounting work. For decades after, punch cards were used in the home office to administer payroll, and in the Ordinary Policy Department to manage premiums, commissions, loans and dividends.

Opposite: Collating punch cards on an IBM computer in the 1950s. All-electronic IBM machines were first introduced to the company in 1949.

company thinks, plans, markets and sells, it also has altered how it communicates and distributes. Prudential has begun, therefore, to develop technological systems that allow it to deliver all forms of products and service in a variety of ways: over the phone and via the Internet as well as face-to-face.

One of the most visible examples of such technological innovations has been LaunchPad, which in 1998 provided all 10,000 Prudential agents with a laptop computer, allowing the sales force to bring investment and insurance planning models to the point of sale. Within a span of months, production among a sampling of agents skyrocketed 150 percent.

In conjunction with the LaunchPad program, Prudential began to compile comprehensive customer databases as contact tools. The databases allow the sales force immediate access to a record of all the business each client does

East Meets West

The tale of Prudential's move to Los Angeles is actually made up of two stories. The first and most obvious describes how opening Prudential's Western Home Office reflected the first step in the company's daring decentralization that began in the mid-1940s. That story would—and most certainly did—find itself prominently featured on the front pages of many business sections. But there's another story, perhaps relegated to the Sunday supplement, but compelling nonetheless. It concerns families leaving loved ones, long train rides and budding romances, doing a day's work in an open-air office— and learning to live with those pesky tar pits.

Getting people to leave Newark wasn't a great challenge—not surprising, perhaps, considering the glamour surrounding Los Angeles in the late 1940s. One story goes that a Prudential employee had initially decided not to relocate but slipped once too often on an icy Newark sidewalk and was on her way in a matter of weeks.

The move wasn't all glitz and sunshine, however. Moving entire families and their belongings cross-

Above: The Montgomery family checks in at the Normandie Hotel, one of many in Los Angeles where employees and their families stayed until they could settle into their new homes.

Opposite: Prudential chose bustling Wilshire Boulevard as the location for its Western Home Office.

with Prudential as well as other pertinent information that might indicate cross-selling opportunities. One Prudential has taken these databases company-wide. Starting in 1998, Prudential began building a client data warehouse, to which all marketing groups have access. Armed with this valuable information, Prudential's marketers can predict what policies might benefit from upgrades or additional products from any Prudential business unit.

The Prosperous International Operations.
When companies undergo massive change, they have a tendency to alter everything. Prudential wisely avoided this trap by measuring each change against the company's new focus and identity—by ensuring, in short, that the intent behind every change was better customer service and satisfaction. This strategy allowed some units to remain largely as they had been. Prudential in particular found that its international insurance

country in the age before dependable air travel presented an enormous logistical challenge. So Prudential hired Jan Bout, a veteran of the Army Transportation Corps, to oversee the company's western migration. At times, he must have longed for the trenches of France. In his book *From Three Cents a Week* ..., William Carr provided the following account:

"During 1948, 522 employees and 644 dependents moved from Newark to Los Angeles—and, thanks to Bout, not a single passenger ever got lost, nor one piece of baggage misplaced. The Pru also moved 150 van loads and 12 full freight-car loads of household effects. Sixty freight cars brought 240 automobiles across the continent. ...

"For those who went by train, it was an exciting trip. The departure was a ceremonial event. Friends, relatives, neighbors, and office colleagues would gather at the Pennsylvania Station in Newark for prolonged, tearful, laughing farewells. Top officers of the company would put in an appearance to wish the departing troops Godspeed. [Prudential Medical Director] Dr. [Robert] Domm, who had gone back to Newark in order to escort one trainload of 'Pioneers,' as they came to be called, said, 'We left Newark on a steaming day in August. I can still remember, 26 years later, how [Prudential President Carrol] Shanks stood there on the platform, ramrod straight, melting in a starched collar. ...'

"On every train there was a party atmosphere, with sing-alongs, games, and jokes to while away the time. Some people drank, some played cards, some entertained the kids. A number of romances got their start on those trips, for about a third of the people were unmarried. Some marriages eventually resulted."

The location committee had purchased land for the new building along Wilshire Boulevard, immediately adjacent to the famous La Brea Tar Pits. In fact, the tar pits actually ran beneath the land on which the building would stand. Therefore, the committee was told, instead of driving pilings to form a foundation, the builders would have to "float" the offices on a concrete slab, a construction that acted like a giant shock absorber when earthquakes struck in 1952 and 1971, preventing a great deal of damage. In 1963, the tar pits provided another benefit: Prudential employees got an impromptu paleontology lesson when from beneath the building emerged the bones of an ancient sloth and birds about 14,000 years old.

Those weren't the only adventures. Carr wrote: "On April 26, 1948, the fifth floor was occupied—although the windows had not yet been installed. 'People had to put rocks on the papers on their desk so that the breeze wouldn't blow them away,' [one employee said]. 'We'd watch the fog roll in one window and out the other.'"

Finally, with the official opening set for November 15, the company invited the public to an open house. More than 10,000 visitors took advantage of the invitation to tour Prudential's fine new building—with glass in every window and not a giant sloth in sight.

business—which had from its inception distinguished itself in customer service—could be left undisturbed.

Prudential intentionally designed its international unit as a "local market abroad." If anything, the division's emphasis on building face-to-face customer relationships and customized needs-based insurance planning closely resembled the Prudential of the 1950s. Most importantly—it has worked.

While Prudential of Japan created the company's international insurance model, the company's 1991 expansion into Korea tested its portability. After a rough start, Prudential of Korea first turned a profit in 1996. It also distinguished itself among its clients. According to an independent 1998 customer survey, POK earned high marks for customer expectations, quality satisfaction, perceived value and customer loyalty.

MARCEL IDIART

Prudential's global expansion has paralleled the many geopolitical and economic changes in the international market.

What I have done throughout my career is basically advise the financial advisors. There have been numerous situations over the years where I have felt like I was really helping someone. I remember back in the 1970s when we had an office in Monte Carlo, and there was a financial advisor there who handled the Vatican account. I remember one day when he called me. He was really worried that he had blown it on an exchange offer because he had missed the dates for the tendering of shares. I called him back and told him he could still tender it on a cash basis. Well, he did it, and then he sent me a nice, complimentary letter, telling me how we had saved the Vatican $200,000 to $300,000.

Marcel Idiart, New York, New York

The Japanese and Korean operations illustrate Prudential International's wise decision to concentrate on service and productivity rather than size. When measured by productivity, Prudential of Japan has been without rival. During the fiscal years 1994 to 1996, life planners in Japan averaged $18 million in face amount—each—per year. Giant Nippon Life was a distant second at $4.4 million per agent. In 1997, 35 percent of Prudential's life planners in Japan qualified for the Million Dollar Round Table, more than three times as many as the company's closest Japanese competitors. In addition, the unit's in-force amount of life insurance has increased nearly a hundredfold in 10 years.

Building upon these successes, Prudential International Insurance has continued to expand. By 1997, Prudential had established additional insurance operations in Taiwan and Brazil.

When I first became a life planner, I met a very capable man. He was very busy, and it took three telephone calls before we finally met. I prepared a plan for him, but he did not call back, and I thought he was not interested. About a week later, however, there was his voice on my answering machine. He wanted to finalize the contract. But he did not come to our scheduled meeting. I called his company; he had died the previous day.

The message on the answering machine haunted me: "I want insurance. The beneficiary will be my aged mother. Please go see my friend, too."

I had this pitiful feeling. I had not been able to do anything for him or his family. I could not work for a week. But a week later, I went to see his friend, and I was able to help him.

Today, I work from 7 in the morning to 11 at night. I work hard with pride because there are so many people who are waiting for me to help them. That memory keeps me working.

Weon Il Choi, Seoul, Korea

Weon Il Choi, with client Dr. Song Jun Do.

Businesses in Argentina, Poland and the Philippines followed.

Taking Asset and Money Management Overseas. Throughout the 1990s, Prudential's other businesses also expanded their international presence. Prudential investment offices—including institutional real estate, private equity and investment trusts—have been established in 11 countries. Early in the next decade, Prudential Global Asset Management, operated by a centralized portfolio management team in London, expected to begin an investment program designed to make private equity investments in the Czech Republic, Hungary, Poland and other Eastern European countries.

On the other side of the globe, Prudential Asset Management Asia completed in June 1998 the third and final closing for one of its most ambitious private equity funds to date, Prudential Asia Private Equity Limited Partnership II. The

The Prudential Connections program brings together individuals from the company's various business units in 36 cities across the country. Together, these people work on projects ranging from cross-marketing to volunteer initiatives on both a local and national scale.

DARCY TODIA

One day in May 1999, I got a call from the manager of the securities galleria office in Houston. He required some help. Public finance in New York was preparing a request for a proposal that had to go out in about a week on a $200 million bond offering for the Fort Bend Independent School District, located in Sugar Land, Texas, the then site of Prudential HealthCare's service center. The school district's RFP had six questions. One of the six was on what Prudential had done for the community in Fort Bend and, specifically, for the school district.

My job, running a Prudential Connection in its Community Affairs Department, makes it imperative for me to know everything that's going on in the Houston area. I knew that I could deliver what they needed. As soon as I had hung up the telephone, I sent an e-mail to the four Prudential associates most active in Fort Bend community affairs.

$540 million fund was the largest non-Japanese entity of its kind ever to invest solely in Asia. Moreover, Prudential Real Estate Investors' global real estate unit, Global Realty Advisors (GRA; Singapore), the asset manager for Prudential's real estate ventures in Asia, emerged from the Asian economic crisis of the late 1990s as a leader in the market, demonstrating its ability to manage effectively under adversity and develop strategies to capitalize on current conditions.

A Tradition of Corporate Citizenship. Business strategy, growth and the bottom line are of utmost concern to Prudential but not to the exclusion of other important matters. Its history as a corporate citizen— providing the less fortunate with, in John Dryden's words, "dignity and security"—could easily fill a book itself. From its early days as the Widows and Orphans Society, Prudential existed as a comforting force within its original community of Newark. As the company

We quickly developed an extraordinary two-page review of Prudential's community affairs activities in Fort Bend. Without changing a word, I forwarded it to Prudential Securities, which was able to get the proposal out on time.

A few weeks later, the members of Houston Connections got some wonderful news. Prudential had been selected to handle part of the business, resulting in $120,000 in commissions and fees. When asked if our input had helped, I learned that it was the deciding factor. The school district was impressed with Prudential. We had the best RFP and, after bidding for six years, we finally won the business.

All of us on the Houston Connections team felt great, and I was thrilled to have been able to coordinate the effort. It was the first documented win attributed to community affairs.

Darcy Todia, Houston, Texas

A Prudential Connections meeting in Houston in 1998 brought together a variety of Prudential employees. *Clockwise:* Brenda Thomas (Prudential Healthcare), Jim Bonow (Prudential Texas Properties & Connections co-chair), John Hinman (Prudential Securities), Paul Bobal (Prudential Securities & Marketing Alliance Committee chair), Ron Doughty (Government Affairs), Jack Horner (Prudential Investments), and Grace Healy (Connections Chicago).

has expanded worldwide, its commitment to making contributions to the lives of individuals and communities has become stronger than ever.

Prudential's corporate citizenship has grown more focused and, in the most positive way, institutionalized—as essentially a part of today's Prudential as any of its business units. From a modest beginning under former CEO Don MacNaughton, Prudential's community resources department has grown into a sophisticated and

powerful social force. Over the past 25 years, the company's citizenship initiatives have been reflected in its three basic divisions: The Prudential Foundation, Social Investments, and Local Initiatives.

Prudential's Continued Partnership with Newark. Prudential's devotion to its communities has never been more evident than in its 125-year relationship with Newark. After the Newark riots of the late 1960s, the company's

Fun for Prudential's Good Samaritans

Prudential employees have always made themselves a part of the community outside their office walls. Company-sponsored extracurricular activities have, likewise, helped create a strong sense of community within Prudential itself.

Perhaps the best evidence of employee fellowship has been the company's annual Excursion Day from Newark to Asbury Park, New Jersey. Begun in 1918, the trip quickly became a tradition. Each year, on into the 1970s, hundreds of Prudential employees boarded trains and buses for a day at the beach, highlighted by the crowning of Miss Excursion Day.

But employees gathered more often than annually. Many of the first clubs that met regularly revolved around athletics. The Prudential Athletic Association was officially founded in 1911, but Prudential teams were fielded before the turn of the century. A 1932 company publication listed among its sports and activities: baseball, basketball, bowling, boxing, wrestling, chess and checkers, riflery, fishing, golf, handball, pool, billiards, shuffleboard, soccer, swimming, tennis, volleyball and walking. Prudential's support of women's athletic teams is noteworthy, sponsoring track, basketball, bowling and softball early on.

For the convenience of Prudential employees, a recreation area was created on the mezzanine of the Washington Street Building. Men and women gathered for cards, dances and dance lessons, table tennis and shuffleboard. The Gibraltar Building contained a gym for practices, workouts and competitions.

Employee-produced cultural events were also popular. Recalling "The Good Old Days" in the *Home Office News* of April 1935, one Prudential employee noted, "Any Prudential man or woman who ever worked with me in any stage

For Men Only

A.A.U. BOXING

OCTOBER 28 1930

8:30 P. M.

IN OUR GYMNASIUM

Three Four-Man Classes—112 to 145 Pounds

11 BOUTS

TWO—SPECIAL MATCHES—TWO

33 ROUNDS OF BOXING

General Admission, 50c   Reserved Seats, 75c

Top: Members of the Policy, Industrial Claim and Medical Departments on the beach at Asbury Park in 1928. *Above:* Members of the Athletic Association tested their boxing skills against opponents from outside the company in the Gibraltar Building Gym.

decision to remain in the city followed a highly emotional debate within the company. Many wanted to follow the lead of other corporations that, during that period and later, left their urban homes for more commodious suburban "campuses." Prudential has remained loyal to its home and in fact has moved several thousand workers back to its Newark offices.

Prudential continues to be both a resource and a stabilizing factor for the city. In 1996, for example, Prudential provided a $1 million challenge grant that promised to double all other donations to Newark's public schools, specifically earmarking early-childhood education programs, magnet schools and professional development programs.

Prudential has also helped Newark become a more culturally rich city, and its support of the arts has gone far beyond putting its name on a plaque. In 1997, Prudential's donation helped build the New Jersey Performing Arts Center, and

production, orchestra or choir work knows the pleasure and satisfaction we derived from our efforts." The Prudential Orchestra and Chorus performed Gilbert and Sullivan's *Mikado* in 1915. In the late 1930s and early 1940s, the home office male chorus sang on CBS Radio on Christmas Eve.

Club activities have long been part of Prudential's commitment to community service. As early as 1916, the Prudential Athletic Association staged shows to benefit the Babies Hospital. During World War II, the Prudential Servicemen's Revue toured camps and bases, logging 7,300 miles and playing before 100,000 servicemen. The show was revived at the request of the Army after the war as the Servicemen's Musical Review, and 90 volunteers visited military bases, hospitals and relief organizations.

The sense of camaraderie doesn't end with retirement parties at Prudential. Retirees continue to participate in activities through the Prudential Retired Employees Association and Retirees Offering Community Service.

Members of the Servicemen's Musical Revue cast during a performance, ca. 1944.

further grants co-endowed a foundation to buy and plan properties around the arts center. The company saw the center as more than an elegant concert venue. It also saw a means to create civic pride and make all of Newark a better place to live and work.

The Arts Center's construction has spawned other efforts to improve city life as people have begun to see evidence that Newark needn't fall victim to its blighted past. The nonprofit organization Connection Newark, whose chairwoman is Pat Ryan, the wife of Prudential's CEO, was created to build private and public community-improvement partnerships and coordinate a steadily increasing number of other development projects. "When I arrived, everyone talked about how bad Newark was," Pat Ryan said. "It's been a privilege to help make a change."

Employee Support and Development. Prudential has also remained generous to its most

Opposite: Agent M. S. "Bob" Olson of the St. Paul Eastview District Office meets with members of the Niederkorn family for a premium collection, 1956.
Below: One of the top priorities of agents through the years has been the comfort of policyholders. Agents visit customers in homes, offices— practically anywhere.

N *o profession has an impact on people like insurance other than teachers and doctors. We change lives. Because of what we do mortgages are paid off, people are able to retire with dignity, children are educated, and last expenses are paid for families who otherwise wouldn't have had the money from their group benefits.*
We make such a difference.

Ina Liss, Norristown, Pennsylvania

immediate community: its employees. In 2000, the company made its 11th appearance in 15 years in *Working Mother* magazine's "100 Best Companies for Working Mothers" list, achieving the recognition as one of the Ten Best Companies in 2000. The magazine cited the company's rich array of work/life programs in helping to raise employee productivity and commitment by reducing stress and absenteeism, providing options for where and when work is done, and the

high return on investment of Prudential's work/life programs. These include daycare and fitness centers, Prudential's LifeWorks resource and referral service, the alternative work arrangement program, its Employee Assistance Program, its generous leave-of-absence policies, and programs available to employees' children such as scholarships.

For the first time in 1999, *Working Woman* magazine named Prudential to their prestigious

list of the Top 25 Companies for Executive Women. The magazine lauded Prudential's efforts in meeting the needs of working women and all employees. The article noted the increasing percentage of female vice presidents at Prudential from 21 to 26 percent since 1994 and the fact that three women are represented on Prudential's Board of Directors. Ten percent of senior managers' pay is linked to the advancement of women they oversee, and flexible work options are the norm, not the exception. In addition, for the past three years, more than half of the entering classes of high-potential management associates have been women.

Training for the future human resources, such as technology, is contributing greatly toward Prudential's preparation for the future. Like practically every other company in America, Prudential's culture has changed by both necessity and design. Twenty-five years ago,

Above: An example of one of the gargoyles, or grotesques as they are more properly called, that adorned the Prudential Building.
Opposite: Completed in 1892, the Prudential Building was designed by architect George Post. The 11-story building required five million bricks and 12 miles of beams, girders and iron posts that composed 114,000 square feet of space.

News, Chet Huntley told this story: "Stern has become a part-time art dealer, and during the past year, he has sold about 260 gargoyles, wrenched from the crumbling walls [of the old Prudential buildings in Newark]. His customers have ranged from prosperous businessmen to schoolteachers, like this lady, who bought a sinister 600-pound number for about $40 because she 'always wanted one.'

"The company warns that these are merely decorative pieces. Although they were imported from Europe, gargoyles are really just horrible-looking rainspouts, designed to ward off evil spirits while carrying water from the eaves. But the folks impulsive enough to plunk down cold, hard cash to cart these grotesque

From Prudential Building Rubble to Conversation Pieces

When the grand old Prudential Building was demolished after 60 years in the heart of Newark, people seemed to want a piece of this rock, too. To be specific, they wanted its gargoyles, which adorned Prudential's Main, West, and North Buildings. E.D. Stern of the Cleveland Wrecking Company supervised the demolition and, along the way, developed something of a second career: gargoyle broker. One night, on the NBC Evening

creatures home are certainly entitled to call them gargoyles.

"The people who buy gargoyles place them on the floors of their living rooms as combination conversation pieces and things to stumble over. Others put them in their gardens to cheer up the flowers. At any rate, the supply of gargoyles is running low. Last week, Mr. Stern's stock was reduced to 30 when a lady stopped and purchased one to send as a valentine."

"Mother Pru" watched over you, even fed you a free lunch. As the century came to a close, Prudential—the perhaps soon-to-be stock company—knew that Wall Street wouldn't let it be Mother Pru any longer.

The human resources department has been instrumental in creating a new cultural model, a blend of market-driven realities leavened with a touch of Mother Pru. While the company seeks to to imbue its employees with a sense of community

responsibility and pride in the organization, it has also taken steps to create what a senior Human Resources executive called "a climate of personal responsibility and development" to accommodate a new "high-change environment."

New forms of training have played an essential role not only in changing the culture but also in instilling the basic cultural traits necessary to support One Prudential. A quarter-century ago, no training at Prudential addressed

the benefits of partnership. Training was based exclusively on obtaining specific skill sets. Today, customer-focused, cross-functional teamwork is the critical concept underlying all training.

The most demonstrable evidence of Prudential's commitment to new learning strategies was the 1998 opening of the Prudential Center for Learning and Innovation in Norwalk, Connecticut. According to a company representative, "The center is the primary place

for Prudential staff to establish new ways of doing business within the company, to gain skills to better lead the organization and to discover strategies that will add value for our customers."

The most significant component in Prudential's recent cultural change initiatives was "One Prudential Exchange," a training program designed to create a new business literacy. Custom-designed "teaching maps" addressed such issues as where Prudential is going

We waive premiums on policies for people who have been disabled for a period of time. In 1995, we received a claim from a policyholder, indicating that she had been disabled since 1972. Kathy Hawkins handled the claim at Prudential. The claimant provided us with medical documentation supporting her claim, and $2,000 of premiums were returned to her. But she had to keep her monthly income at a certain point to continue to qualify for her Social Security benefits, so she promptly sent the check back, saying she did not want to lose her benefits. Kathy made calls to Social Security and a number of other agencies who said she could keep the check, provided she spent it within the month she received it. The woman was so grateful. She accepted the money and went out and filled her freezer with food for her family.

Donna Strohm, Dresher, Pennsylvania

It takes a team of adjusters and account representatives, in addition to field representatives, to meet the insurance needs of Prudential customers.

and why, how each unit on the organizational chart relates to the others and the effects of Prudential's mission and identity on business strategy. Furthermore, and perhaps most importantly, the program emphasized how and why change takes place within all aspects of the company, from its mission, to marketing and product development.

Prudential Today ... and Into the Next Century. Prudential's training programs reflect a company that values its employees and wants to give them skills and knowledge to excel. They are among the Prudential initiatives that also reflect the sentiment in an Art Ryan quote from a 1998 company publication: "At this heightened level of competition, satisfactory isn't good enough." As the 1990s came to an end, the company's renewed stability allowed it to focus once again on being far more than satisfactory.

For Prudential, being "more than

TOMOMI NISHIKAWA

I have been working for Prudential for eight years and have seen how we help people in need— even in my own family. My wife's younger brother decided to get a policy when he got married. Months later, his spine was severely injured during rugby practice. He was taken to the hospital where it was discovered that he was paralyzed. This happened when he was 30, only 10 months after his marriage and 4 months after he had received a policy. He had wanted to go with a Japanese insurance company, but my wife convinced him to go with Prudential. He remained in the hospital for a year and a half. Right now, he is back in the hospital, but he does not have to worry about his life financially. Next year, he is having his house renovated!

Tomomi Nishikawa, Tokyo, Japan

Agent Charlene Chen of Prudential of Taiwan, after working an 11-hour day, meets with a prospect to discuss his insurance needs.

satisfactory" means preparing for new competitors and providing exemplary customer service. Technology remains critical in both these areas, particularly as the Internet expands channels of distribution. A company officer stated, "Our competition is anyone who can open a Web site." The Internet has also affected customer buying habits. "The Internet is all about what I want," noted another senior executive. "If a potential customer doesn't like what they see,

you're a click away from oblivion."

For a company that has based more than a century of success on building face-to-face relationships, such notions are daunting. The company has wisely channeled its efforts toward continuing to build those relationships—only now through a combination of channels. The definition of "face to face" has changed.

Prudential Real Estate provides a striking example of how technology can be used to

Carrol Shanks: "I Like the Action, the Battle, the Campaigns"

As any wise leader will tell you, tradition is a noble concept, but tradition must always be measured against the unsentimental yardstick of utility. "That's the way we've always done it" can too often be the last words shouted before the ship goes under. It's doubtful that Carrol Shanks ever uttered them.

Opposite: Carrol Shanks (far right) with Prudential Vice President Charles Campbell (left) and Jacksonville Mayor Haydon Burns (center), at the groundbreaking for the South Central Home Office, May 16, 1953.

Perhaps Shanks' disregard for tradition —particularly traditional business thinking— sprang from his upbringing. His background could hardly have been more different from his predecessors. Up to this point in Prudential's history, the company had essentially been run by Drydens for the first half of its life and Princetonians for the rest. Both elements had mostly been exemplars of all that was good about Prudential. But times had changed and so had the company. And Carrol Shanks wasn't interested in being a custodian.

Shanks wasn't an Easterner. His roots were Midwestern—and even then, they were not in the soft verdure of Ohio or Indiana but the less-forgiving climes of Minnesota. He did boyhood time in Idaho, where his father had moved in a failed attempt at farming and where, to help support the family, young Shanks worked in a brickyard. Instead of the Ivy League, it was the University of Washington, where he graduated Phi Beta Kappa in 1921. He then proceeded to Columbia Law School and later taught there and at Yale, specializing in corporate finance.

Finding teaching too removed from the action, he joined Prudential in 1932. Walking into his new job, eager to apply his

enhance the customer relationship. In the first half of 1999, agents began using customized Palm Pilot VII handheld computers with wireless modems, giving them instant access—anytime, anywhere—to multiple listings, lists of houses within a certain price range or location, and related market and mortgage information. Developing the Palm Pilot capability illustrates Prudential's increased desire to become a technological leader by taking risks with cutting-

edge hardware, software and networking systems.

Likewise, Prudential Securities is developing strategies for using cellular telephones as databases, allowing brokers to access information, communicate it to customers and make transactions anywhere. Customer service representatives at Pru Advisor Call Centers are able to instantly access complete customer profiles as well as product information from every business unit while customers are on the phone.

considerable knowledge of corporate finance, he must have felt like a fat man in a bakery. However, the Depression was taking its toll: Corporations were going bankrupt by the hundreds. Shanks' job was to salvage what he could from these bankruptcies. From the beginning, his methods illustrated how much he prized innovation and creativity over lockstep procedure. As William Carr described in his book *From Three Cents a Week* ...: "He once swapped $200,000 in virtually worthless railroad bonds for 200 miles of railroad track, and then sold the steel rails for $60,000 in cash."

Yet Shanks was hardly a wild man. Carr put it well: "He looked austere, aloof, somewhat forbidding—'glacial' was an adjective often applied to him. ... To most of the world, he was the epitome of a 19th-century, Calvinistic banker; but inside, he harbored the fiery passions of an adventurer, a revolutionary." Moving into the postwar era, Prudential needed both qualities, and in Carrol Shanks, it got them.

During Shanks' 15-year stewardship, Prudential grew to become the nation's—if not the world's—largest seller of life insurance. Prudential's annual sales increased from a little less than $2 billion in 1945 to almost $10 billion in 1960. Shanks stepped down from Prudential's presidency in 1960. He died in 1976.

New strategic planning procedures ensure that these improvements won't be isolated ones. Today, all initial stages of business planning include technical experts who develop integrated and interactive cross-functional application platforms. Technology is now a partner in the planning process—One Prudential at its technological best.

On the Horizon: the Prospect of Demutualization. At the close of this account, it seems appropriate and encouraging to contemplate an event that can be seen both as a fitting conclusion to the past quarter-century and an exciting prospect for the future. In February 1998, Prudential began to explore full demutualization.

With so many promising initiatives up and running and with a healthy bottom line, why demutualize? Prudential's consideration of this issue has centered on one primary question: Is the mutual structure still appropriate for a company

*W*hen I started six years ago, I called on a guy who happened to be a neighbor of mine. It was a $5,000 policy. I reviewed the policy with him, and we agreed that he needed more insurance, but he had Hodgkin's disease, and he was afraid he was uninsurable. Sure enough, he was.

As a result of starting the relationship with him, though, I was able to insure his wife. Soon after that, he became quite sick, and we did a lot of service on his policy, loaning money out of it but keeping it in place for the death benefit.

He died two months later, and his wife called me to go over his policy. In reviewing the materials in his desk, we found some policies through his union and through his work. We even found a policy through Reader's Digest. When we had reviewed all his stuff— it took almost a week—we found $240,000 that she had no idea he had. She is still one of my best clients.

Ray Dewey, Richmond, Virginia

Opposite: A Jacksonville, Florida, agent talks with a family in 1954. The tradition of caring and friendship among Prudential's agents is part of what has made them the leaders in their field worldwide.

of Prudential's size and type in this business environment at this point in time? None of the criteria favoring the 1915 mutualization exists any longer. Participating mutual products designed for policyholders—such as whole life— now account for only 15 percent of total sales, and, in fact, all life insurance brings in only 50 percent of total company revenue. One executive described the situation: "We're a financial services organization wearing the shell of a mutual insurance company."

Moreover, recent external developments favor demutualization even more. For example, on November 12, 1999, President Clinton signed into law legislation to drop most of the legal barriers separating banks, brokerages and insurance companies, a move that will inevitably increase competition for organizations like Prudential. Access to capital, such as stock, provides an enormous hedge against these

competitive pressures, as former CEO Bob Winters noted, "Corporate acquisitions of $20 billion are no longer all that unusual, and an acquirer who doesn't have stock as currency is just not going to be able to stay in the game."

As writing on this book came to a conclusion, a final decision on demutualization had not been reached. The company's performance—as well as the atmosphere on Wall Street—could certainly affect its timing. Prudential, wisely, is not racing

into the matter.

If Prudential demutualizes, more challenges await. Under the direct pressure of the stock market, Prudential, always a great seller, must continue efforts to become a top-notch marketer. Planning and budgeting will become far more important in the daily life of the organization. And Prudential, for the first time, will have to learn to deal with quarterly public scrutiny.

However, demutualization also holds plenty of

Elvera Fernandez with Sergio Mercado during a tutoring session. The program partners children of Latino heritage with role models of similar backgrounds in an effort to prevent kids from dropping out of school.

JIMMIE GONZALEZ

About 6 years ago, I realized Prudential needed to view the Hispanic community as a viable business market. In 40 years, the Hispanic population will make up approximately 25 percent of the U.S. population. Prudential was not tapping into ethnic consumer markets and would have missed profitable business opportunities. I felt Prudential's ethnic associates could help understand and enter their representative markets. Being of Hispanic descent, I contacted other Hispanic executives at Prudential and proposed the Hispanic Heritage Network (HHN) to facilitate communication between Prudential and the Hispanic community. The HHN was conceived in 1995.

HHN's main goal is to focus attention on the potential business value of rapidly growing ethnic communities.

Progress has been swift. Through December 2000, HHN had approximately 300 members participating in various community activities, including tutoring, voter registration, census counting, toy drives and walk-a-thons. HHN recently

benefits. In addition to increased access to capital, demutualization can help define Prudential's identity as a financial services powerhouse. Demutualization will not only accelerate the One Prudential process, it will also form its capstone. Nothing will make both employees and the public think of Prudential as one financial services company like having the same stock quote. "That stock quote gets us into the public arena," one executive said. "It

becomes our score card."

Whether the company demutualizes or not, the newly stabilized and forward-looking Prudential is putting the pieces into place. The history of the past quarter-century ends with exciting challenges as the company looks toward a prosperous future. Prudential stands primed for fresh innovations and opportunities, but, as throughout its history, it does so with the same values and priorities that The Rock was founded

*initiated a bimonthly mentoring session at the Rafael
Hernandez School, in which associates are mentors and
tutors to Hispanic children. In addition, HHN coordinates
Prudential's Hispanic Heritage Month celebrations,
represents Prudential at external Hispanic events and
conducts internal mentoring circles.*

*Although HHN has made tremendous strides in its
community and diversity efforts, it inches toward its major
goal: to help Prudential capitalize fully on the potential
business opportunities lying dormant in the U.S. ethnic
market sectors, totaling about $1.2 trillion. Hopefully,
future associates will see this cause to its culmination.*

Jimmie Gonzalez, Newark, New Jersey

on 125 years ago. A recent statement by CEO Art
Ryan demonstrates that steadfastness of spirit:
"We pledge to be there for our customers and
clients when they need us most. We work hard to
be a good neighbor. And we take pride in
consistently delivering on our promises."

Women in the
Workplace

When recounting the history of the American working woman, the temptation is to keep it tidy: A century ago, women had few options, and now things are better. But the real story is less linear and logical than one might suppose.

When Prudential was founded in 1875, work options for women were limited. A married woman working outside the home signaled domestic distress, and companies refrained from hiring married women because they didn't want to threaten family stability. Prudential acted likewise, having an iron-clad rule that if a woman got married, she lost her job.

Nevertheless, one of Prudential's first agents was a woman—and a married one at that. Julia Babbitt started with the Pru in 1876, and remained an agent until her retirement in 1912, securing jobs at Prudential for her husband and son along the way.

While single women were employable at the home office, they could still expect only limited advancement and wages below subsistence level. Their appearance was also tightly governed. Women at Prudential were not permitted to wear makeup of any kind; short-sleeved blouses

PRECEDING PAGE: A SWITCHBOARD OPERATOR AT THE SOUTH CENTRAL HOME OFFICE IN JACKSONVILLE, FLORIDA, 1955. ABOVE: THE HOME OFFICE CLERICAL STAFF, 1888. OPPOSITE (CLOCKWISE): AN AGENTS' OUTING, ca. 1900; WAR PRODUCTION IN THE HOME OFFICE, NEWARK, NEW JERSEY, DURING WORLD WAR II; AN EMPLOYEE OPERATING A TELEVOICE WRITER, 1954.

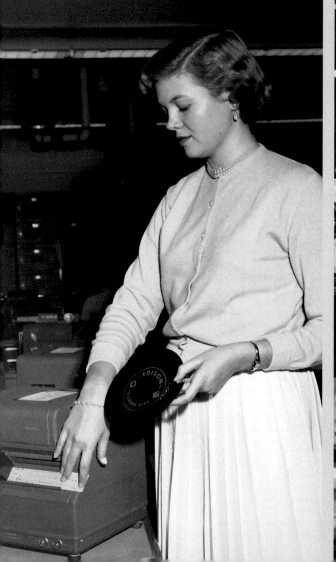

were outlawed, and skirts were expected to reach the ankles.

By the 1920s, increased educational opportunities enabled women to enter a profession by choice rather than necessity, which lessened the stigma of being a "working woman." But within the workplace, changes were hardly radical. Women's restrooms were patrolled for smokers, and married and pregnant women were still dismissed.

OPPOSITE: TRAINEES FROM THE NEWLY ESTABLISHED SCHO ARRIVE IN NEWARK, NEW JERSEY, JUNE 1953. *ABOVE:* THE HOME OFFICE IN NEWARK, ca. 1940s. *BELOW:* EXCURSION DAY AT ASBURY PARK, NEW JERSEY, 1935.

The role of women at companies such as Prudential was an ambiguous one. While women's athletic teams and contests stressed strength and agility, company beauty pageants, complete with swimsuit competitions, stressed women's decorative nature.

But then came World War II, which can be seen as the greatest equal rights opportunity in American history. As men served on the front line, women served on the assembly line. At Prudential, women held jobs previously reserved for men. Staffing issues ultimately forced the company to temporarily abandon its marriage

OPPOSITE (CLOCKWISE): THE TYPEWRITING DEPARTMENT, NEWARK, NEW JERSEY, 1888; ANNA GARCIA (STANDING, CENTER) CONDUCTS A TOUR OF THE GIBRALTAR LABORATORY, 1971; JEAN SHIRLEY COMPETES AT A PICAA TRACK MEET IN PHILADELPHIA, PENNSYLVANIA, ca. 1920s. *ABOVE (FROM LEFT):* MISS EXCURSION DAY CONTEST WINNER CAROL ESDALE (SECOND FROM RIGHT) WITH RUNNERS-UP AT ASBURY PARK, NEW JERSEY, 1969; A HABITAT FOR HUMANITY HOME-BUILDING PROJECT, ca. 1990s.

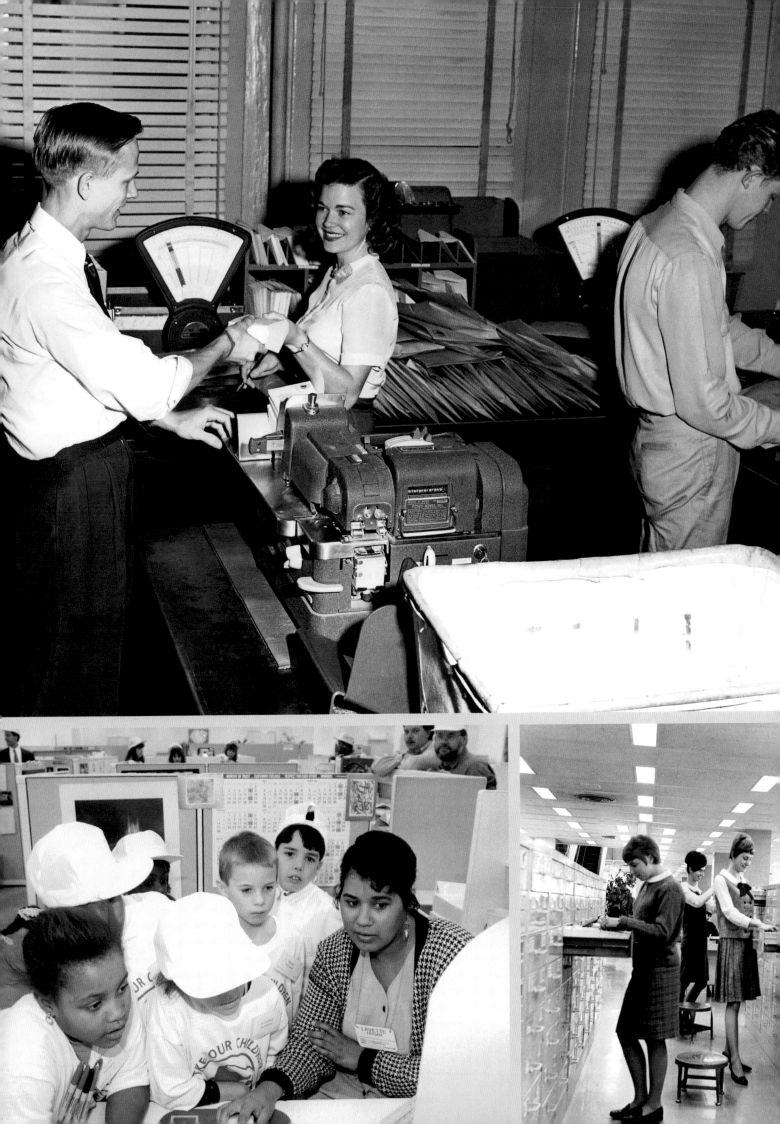

restrictions, a policy that became permanent in 1948.

A generation after the war, the women's movement brought sweeping change to the workplace. In 1971, Vice President and Secretary Isabelle Kirchner became the company's first female officer. And in the 1970s, the beauty pageants disappeared from the company's social scene. Today, Prudential is frequently named as a corporate exemplar by Working Mother magazine, a clear indication of how women's presence has transformed Prudential's workplace.

OPPOSITE (CLOCKWISE): THE MAILING DEPARTMENT IN THE SCHO TEMPORARY OFFICE, 1954; THE MAINLAND OFFICE, LINWOOD, NEW JERSEY, ca. 1960s; LAVETTE HOGAN DEMONSTRATES PART OF HER DAILY DUTIES ON "TAKE YOUR CHILDREN TO WORK DAY," 1993. *ABOVE:* A COMPANY-SPONSORED CONFERENCE AT THE EASTERN HOME OFFICE IN NEWARK, NEW JERSEY, ca. 1970.

Charting the Rock's Course

The Prudential Timeline

1839

1839

John Fairfield Dryden is born August 7 in Temple Mills, Maine.

1849

Industrial and General of England becomes the first company to market industrial insurance, a form of insurance for the working class.

1861

Dryden enters Yale University.

1870

The United States Mutual Benefit Company is founded at 112 Broadway in Manhattan. H.H. Goodman is president, and John Dryden, secretary. The company fails to obtain a state charter.

1873

Dryden joins the Widows and Orphans Friendly Society.

1874

The Prudential Life Insurance Company is founded in New York City, but its plan to sell industrial insurance would never get off the ground. Its investors would fail to raise sufficient capital.

1875

The Prudential Friendly Society is formed in Newark, New Jersey.

On October 13, the board of directors meets for the first time and elects Allan Bassett president; John Dryden, secretary; and Isaac Gaston, a bank cashier, treasurer.

William R. Drake becomes the first to apply for industrial insurance through Prudential. That same year, he is elected to the board of directors.

Policy No. 11 is issued on November 15 on the life of Edna Bleye. She lives until September 26, 1957.

Prudential has 284 policies by the end of the year.

1876

Prudential pays its first sickness claim April 11 to Miss Maggie Conover of Newark.

Prudential pays its first death claim May 4 for Industrial Policy No. 724, covering 2-year-old Joseph F. Smith.

Prudential throws its first company party on June 2 to celebrate the sale of its 5,000th policy.

The fraudulent Prudential Benefit Company is exposed and brought before a grand jury. Two Prudential men, John Lyle and S. Lambertson, are implicated in the scandal.

1877

Dryden travels to England to examine Prudential Assurance Company's operating practices. Upon his return, Prudential updates its business practices, discontinuing, for example, its "sickness policies."

PRUDENTIAL ASSURANCE COMPANY, ca. 1960s.

On March 15, the company changes its name to The Prudential Insurance Company of America.

Prudential opens an office at 114 Ellison St. in Paterson, New Jersey.

1878

Prudential moves its main office to the Centennial Building at 215 Market St.

The company begins to expand, opening offices in Jersey City and Elizabeth, New Jersey.

Prudential begins making mortgage loans.

1879

Prudential opens an office in Camden, New Jersey.

Allen Basset resigns as president. Noah F. Blanchard is voted acting president and 12 days later is confirmed as Prudential's full-fledged president.

Facing hard times during the depression that followed the collapse of 1873, Metropolitan Life Insurance Company of America begins to sell industrial life insurance. It begins to compete directly with Prudential when it makes Allen Bassett the superintendent of its Newark district.

Prudential begins moving into New York City and Philadelphia.

Leopold Cahn founds Leopold Cahn & Company, Brokers and Investment Bankers, later to be renamed Bache Securities. The firm would be acquired by Prudential in 1981.

1880

Prudential installs its first telephone.

At the age of 18, Jules Bache joins Leopold Cahn & Co., his uncle's investment firm.

1881

After the death of Prudential President Noah Blanchard, a protracted battle ensues, in which Dryden is elected to the presidency by one vote.

JOHN DRYDEN (RIGHT) AND WILLIAM CARTER, 1888.

1883

Prudential moves its headquarters to the Jube Building at 880 Broad Street.

Jules Bache is made a partner of Leopold Cahn & Co.

Modern statistical methods assume center stage as Prudential establishes its Actuarial Department.

1884

Major developments in communications occur. Prudential creates the Print Department in January, and in July, the first Prudential magazine is published.

On August 4, the company begins to pay all death claims within 24 hours of receiving proof of death.

1885

A million dollars, a million policies: As its assets top $1 million, Prudential issues its millionth industrial policy—to John Dryden.

1886

Prudential establishes its Ordinary Insurance Branch. Dryden purchases the first Prudential ordinary policy on January 19, and the company's first ordinary agency opens on December 9 in Bay Shore on Long Island.

On October 17, Frederick Robothom, head of the Auditors Department, becomes the first employee to die while in Prudential's service.

1887

Prudential pays its first ordinary claim on Policy No. 13: $1,000 on the life of John Anders.

1888

Property at Bank and Broad Streets in Newark is purchased for the construction of Prudential's headquarters. The company had originally bought property on the corner of Broad and Franklin but finally settles on the Bank Street site.

1888

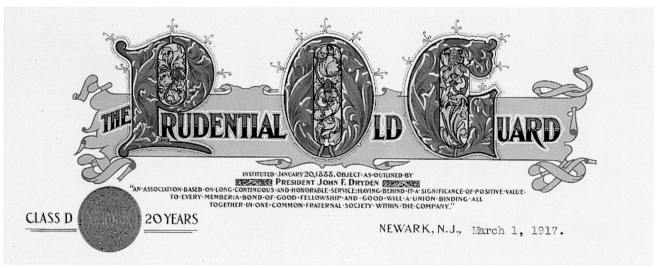

LETTERHEAD, ca. 1920.

Dryden establishes the Prudential Old Guard, honoring men and women who have served the company for five years or more.

The first company rate book is made available.

1890

Leopold Cahn & Company opens a second office in New York City and a third in Albany, New York. It is the first branch established by any brokerage firm with a direct wire link to headquarters.

The Dryden Library is established.

1892

The Prudential Building officially opens December 2. At the time, it is the largest building in New Jersey.

Leopold Cahn & Company is reorganized as J.S. Bache and Company. President Jules Bache is 32 years old.

Prudential discontinues its 3-cent industrial policies as well as its policies written in German.

1895

Prudential installs card-punching machines invented by John K. Gore and built by his brother-in-law. They are used in the valuation of industrial policies. The machine sorts cards by weekly premium at a rate of 15,000 per hour. Once sorted, the cards are counted by another machine.

EMPLOYEES USING GORE CARD-PUNCHING MACHINES.

1896

Prudential debuts a new corporate symbol—the Rock—in a *Leslie's Weekly* advertisement. It appears with the slogan "The Prudential Has the Strength of Gibraltar."

Prudential introduces an incentive program for agents.

1897

A new industrial insurance policy eliminates most differences between ordinary and industrial policyholders.

1898

The battleship *Maine* explodes, killing 253 men, 21 of whom are Prudential policyholders.

Prudential grants a concession to its policyholders, allowing them to serve in the Spanish-American War without having to pay any additional premiums.

1900

Edward Riley sells the company's first $1 million policy.

1901

Prudential constructs four additional buildings as part of the Home Office complex.

1902

Prudential begins its merger with the Fidelity Trust Company, sparking a bitter debate.

Dryden is elected to the U.S. Senate.

1904

The company extends its operations to the Hawaiian islands.

1905

Senator Dryden introduces an insurance regulation bill.

1907

Prudential resumes issuing 3-cent policies.

1909

The company opens its first Canadian office in Toronto.

Prudential issues its millionth ordinary policy.

1910

The *Home Office News* is first published.

1911

John Dryden dies.

The company has 10 million policies in force.

The Home Office Infirmary is established for employees who suffer illness or injury on the job.

THE INFIRMARY LABORATORY, ca. 1930.

1912

Forrest Dryden succeeds his father as Prudential's president.

Prudential distributes $20 million in surplus to its policyholders. The action prompts a lawsuit from Prudential stockholders, who claim that the surplus should have been paid to them.

1913

Prudential begins the process of mutualization.

1914

Harold Bache joins J.S. Bache and Company.

1915

With the exception of a few holdouts, Prudential's majority stockholders sell their stock back to the company. Prudential becomes a mutual company.

1916

The Department of Labor intervenes in a strike by Prudential's New York-area agents.

Prudential announces that it will provide free insurance to its Home Office employees.

1917

1917

The company organizes the Prudential Home Guard, a small Newark-based militia of Prudential employees. While the Home Guard would remain inactive, 1,729 Pru employees serve in the U.S. military during World War I. Fifty would die in action.

Prudential announces that it will pay the salaries of all employees entering war service.

1918

Influenza spreads throughout the world, killing 400,000 to 500,000 in the United States alone. Prudential experiences difficulty in processing claims because so many of its employees are ill.

1919

On March 2, Prudential grants continuous service to all employees who served in the armed forces during World War I.

1920

During a period of feverish investment in New York real estate, Prudential extends a $3 million mortgage to the F.W. Woolworth estate on the Woolworth Building. At the time, the Manhattan landmark was the United States' tallest building.

1922

Forrest Dryden resigns as president. Edward Duffield succeeds him.

Prudential sells its shares of Fidelity Union's stock.

WAR SAVINGS SOCIETY PARADE, 1918.

1923

Prudential issues a group life insurance policy covering the 2,500 officers of the Philadelphia Police Department. The $7 million of coverage is believed to be the largest group life insurance policy issued at the time.

1925

As the company's growth demands innovation, Prudential employees put their ingenuity to work. Emil Mueller and Supervisor McIntyre design and build a machine that will insert carbon paper between Ordinary premium notices and receipts at a speed of 4,000 sets per hour.

1926

Construction is completed on the Gibraltar Building.

THE GIBRALTAR BUILDING, 1926.

1927

The three most common causes of disability among Prudential policyholders are tuberculosis, insanity and cancer, according to a company survey.

1928

As the Texas market for group insurance expands, Prudential is licensed to do business in the Lone Star State.

1930

While other large insurance companies are abandoning the agricultural market, Prudential reports an increase in farm mortgages and loans from 1928 to 1929.

1931

President Duffield tells Prudential employees assembled in Atlantic City that the Great Depression would end in the United States if confidence could be restored. He cites Prudential's record sales volume in 1930 and suggests an even better year in 1931.

THE ROCK, IN DEPRESSION-ERA PARADE, ca. 1933.

Prudential launches a sales campaign that results in a record month: More than a million new life insurance policies are issued in November.

1932

The accidental death benefit provision is liberalized to cover the accidental deaths of fare-paying aircraft passengers.

The Gore card-punching computation machines begin to wear out, and the Powers Division of the Remington Rand Company builds replacement equipment to Prudential's specifications. The new machines can process cards used by the Gore system.

1935

Prudential replaces its Powers/Gore punch card equipment with a new system developed by fledgling IBM.

1936

Prudential's World War I veterans can use their war bonuses to purchase and immediately occupy homes in the New York metropolitan area.

1938

Edward Duffield dies of a cerebral hemorrhage. Franklin D'Olier becomes the sixth president of the company.

1941

1941

The United States enters World War II. Eventually, 6,412 Prudential employees would serve in the military; 111 of them would be killed in action.

COMPANY WAR BOND DRIVE DURING WWII.

More than 9,500 employees—82 percent of Prudential's Newark work force—purchase defense savings bonds in a payroll-deduction plan.

1942

Prudential signs its first union contract.

More than 20,000 Prudential people in 40 states sell war savings stamps to policyholders and the general public.

Women employees are, for the first time, permitted to continue in their positions after marriage. Previously, the company employed only unmarried women. The company would suspend its rule requiring the resignation of female employees about to be married until six months after the end of the war.

Because of war conditions, Prudential increases by 10 percent the working hours and salaries of clerical employees.

The first state health insurance law—the Rhode Island Cash Sickness Compensation Act—takes effect May 10. Employers must collect 1 percent from each employee on salaries up to $3,000. Benefits range from $6.75 to $18 a week.

To improve military morale, the Musical Revue of the Prudential Insurance Company Athletic Association performs for the troops.

The Home Office—as well as any branch offices with five or more typewriters—sells 20 percent of its typewriters to the U.S. government in support of the war effort.

The War Department occupies the Washington Street Building.

1943

President D'Olier presents $100,000 to the Newark chapter of the Red Cross for its war fund.

To alleviate traffic problems, the Newark offices change their office hours. Employees work from 8:10 a.m. to 4:30 p.m. and have 38 minutes for lunch.

Prudential repurchases the final outstanding shares of Prudential stock for $1,500 per share. Members of the Blanchard family are the last to own Prudential stock.

1944

U.S. President Franklin Roosevelt appoints D'Olier as chairman of the Strategic Bombing Survey.

Jules Bache dies. Harold Bache succeeds him, and the firm is renamed Bache & Company.

1945

Prudential announces a new life insurance policy for people buying consumer goods with installment payments. Upon the death of the purchaser, the unpaid balance is cancelled and the merchandise becomes part of the purchaser's estate.

Prudential officials consult with Newark Mayor Vincent Murphy on financing a 25-block, $19 million slum clearance project. The project is the first proposed under the New Jersey Urban Redevelopment Corporation Act.

1946

Franklin D'Olier steps aside as president and becomes chairman of the board of directors. Carrol Shanks is elected Prudential's seventh president.

1947

Prudential introduces the Dollar Guide.

The Western Home Office is established in Los Angeles, and Prudential occupies several office buildings there while the Wilshire Drive headquarters is constructed. Prudential pays all moving expenses for 522 transferred employees and their families. Many travel from the East Coast to the West Coast on Prudential trains.

Prudential moves back into the Washington Street Building, occupied by the War Department since 1942.

PLAQUE PRESENTED BY THE WAR DEPARTMENT, 1947.

A Mark I computer is used for a test of ordinary insurance billing.

1948

Prudential begins a large-scale decentralization. The company would open regional home offices in Los Angeles, Chicago, Minneapolis, Philadelphia, Jacksonville, Houston, Boston and northern New Jersey as well as a Canadian home office in Toronto.

Female employees who get married are no longer required to resign. The company also begins hiring newly married female employees.

The new Western Home Office officially opens November 15. A two-ton piece of the Rock of Gibraltar serves as its cornerstone.

Prudential agrees to purchase a UNIVAC computer for $297,976. However, the contract would be cancelled in 1950—before the computer is delivered.

Franklin D'Olier retires as chairman of the board of directors.

1950

Prudential becomes the first life insurance company to advertise on television, sponsoring "Prudential Family Playhouse."

Prudential celebrates the 75th anniversary of its founding.

The company opens the Canadian Home Office. About 550 employees and trainees are transferred over the Labor Day weekend.

1951

An 81-day work stoppage—the largest white-collar strike in American history—affects Prudential.

On July 1, Prudential's group insurance programs cover about 5.3 million employees. This figure represents a peak in the insurance industry and a gain of 283 percent for Prudential since 1946.

Prudential enters the individual accident and health insurance fields.

1952

1952

Prudential offers limited life insurance policies to military personnel not subject to combat or aviation hazards.

Prudential extends the retirement age of women from 60 to 65 to match that of men, but women retain the option of retiring at 60.

Prudential sets up a Sickness and Accident Department to offer personal health insurance.

The worst earthquake to hit Los Angeles since 1906 causes minor damage at the Western Home Office and gives employees a day off.

General Motors' Group Creditors Policy reaches $1 billion, the largest in insurance history. For a few cents a week, GM car buyers have the assurance that, if they die, their vehicles will be paid off and their families will be given clear title.

Prudential experiments with employees working from 4:30 p.m. to midnight. The workers—mostly married women with family responsibilities—perform simple transcriptions and other clerical tasks. The company hopes to improve service and decrease clerical overtime.

The Southwestern Home Office opens in Houston. Prudential helps finance 200 homes for the transferees.

CELEBRATING THE OPENING OF THE SWHO, 1952.

Frank J. Rady becomes the 20,000th employee in company history to complete 20 years of service.

1953

Air conditioning cools employees in home and field offices.

The company starts a "TV Teaching Aid" series, providing historical background for Prudential's "You Are There" TV show.

The North Central Home Office is established in Minneapolis.

The South Central Home Office is established in Jacksonville, Florida.

1954

Umberto A. Palo, a former high school teacher in South River, New Jersey, joins Prudential as an agent and sells $2.5 million during his first nine months. His sales, a record for individual agents, earn him more than $35,000.

Prudential makes a $250 million loan to Chrysler—Prudential's largest loan to date.

1955

Prudential installs its first large-scale electronic computer.

Prudential dedicates its new Midwestern headquarters in Chicago. The 41-story, 601-foot building is, at the time, the city's tallest building.

To make the transition from a card to a magnetic tape computer system, the information on more than 13 million punch cards is transferred to tape in four weeks.

1956

Prudential begins the demolition of the 1892 Prudential Building at 763 Broad Street.

The family policy is introduced.

1957

Prudential's Twentieth Century television series presents "Where We Stand," a 90-minute program that compares the relative strengths of the United States and the Soviet Union in four primary areas: science, weapons and defense, education, and economics.

CBS NEWS ANCHOR, WALTER CRONKITE.

Prudential opens a Northeastern Home Office in Boston.

1958

Prudential announces plans for a $12 million Toronto headquarters.

1959

As part of a significant urban renewal effort for downtown Newark, Prudential announces a $20 million redevelopment program for its headquarters.

1960

Carrol Shanks resigns as Prudential's president.

Prudential makes a $100 million loan to a financial agency of the Mexican government.

1961

Louis R. Menagh is elected president of the company.

Prudential experiments with an early data transmission system between Boston and Newark. The system would eventually run on a leased telephone line and would transmit 250 characters per second.

Prudential leases space in the Gibraltar Building to the Western Electric and Eastern Air companies.

Prudential purchases the Empire State Building.

THE EMPIRE STATE BUILDING,
NEW YORK, NEW YORK, ca. 1961.

1962

Menagh retires, and Orville Beal becomes Prudential's ninth president.

Prudential sells a building site in San Francisco, putting to rest its plans for an additional regional home office serving the Western states.

1963

Prudential sells dental insurance for the first time.

Prudential joins in a new civil defense program, emphasizing mass survival over individual and family survival. Emergency supplies are stored throughout the Home Office buildings.

Hurricane Dora damages the regional home office in Florida.

COMPANY CIVIL DEFENSE HELMET.

1965

1965

Spring floods and tornadoes in the upper Midwest prompt
the Minneapolis regional home office to run newspaper ads
telling customers how to do business with the company
during the emergency.

The Prudential Center is dedicated in Boston.

THE PRUDENTIAL TOWER, BOSTON,
MASSACHUSETTS, 1965.

1966

Prudential surpasses Metropolitan Life as the largest insurance
company in the United States.

1968

To overcome staffing shortages, the Minneapolis office hires
housewives for filing, service clerk and messenger jobs. Young
men waiting to be drafted fill mail and light manual positions.

1969

Orville Beal retires, and Donald S. MacNaughton becomes the
10th president of the company

Prudential announces plans for a Central Atlantic Home Office in
Fort Washington, Pennsylvania.

Prudential announces plans to finance the construction of the
Gateway Building in Newark as part of a larger Gateway Urban
Renewal Project.

THE GATEWAY ONE BUILDING, NEWARK,
NEW JERSEY.

1970

MacNaughton becomes chairman of the board and chief
executive officer. Kenneth C. Foster is elected president and
chief operating officer.

Prudential becomes the first major insurance company to
market variable annuities to individuals. Agents must be
licensed as registered representatives.

The company establishes the Prudential Property Investment
Separate Account. It is the first open-ended commingled real
estate equity fund designed for U.S. pension plans.

Prudential enters the automobile and homeowner insurance
business through a management contract with the Kemper
Insurance Group.

The Gateway complex opens in Newark. Prudential is one of
its major financiers.

A companywide jobs program hires 250 needy boys and girls for summer jobs.

SUMMER JOBS PROGRAM PARTICIPANTS.

Prudential forms PRUCO, a holding company, to control many of Pru's subsidiaries.

The company makes its first venture into the aviation industry by offering liability insurance to American Airlines.

1971
The Prudential Property and Casualty Insurance Company is founded to underwrite and market automobile and homeowners insurance.

Bache & Company goes public, offering 2.5 million shares of stock, which raise $40 million in capital.

An earthquake causes minor damage to the Western Home Office in Los Angeles. There are no injuries.

Prudential tops $30 billion in assets.

PRUCO Securities begins active trading.

"Get a piece of the Rock" enters the American lexicon with the debut of the famous ad campaign.

Prudential introduces an individual life policy designed for youth, returning war veterans, young parents and college students.

1972
Prudential declares a moratorium on premium payments and waives death certificate requirements in the wake of a major flood in Rapid City, South Dakota.

1973
Prudential assumes management responsibilities for the Rhode Island Group Health Insurance Association—one of the nation's first federally qualified health maintenance organizations.

PruCare of Houston becomes the first federally qualified HMO owned by an insurer.

Bache & Company acquires Halsey, Stuart & Company, one of the nation's leading corporate bond and municipal underwriting houses.

REPRESENTATIVES OF PRUCARE, HOUSTON, TEXAS, 1973.

1973

Prudential expands its reinsurance business by establishing the Prudential Reinsurance Company subsidiary. The company insures pieces of policies sold by other insurance companies. Prudential announces plans to open offices in Guam and Hong Kong.

PRUDENTIAL REINSURANCE SALES AID.

1974

The development of the Advanced Ordinary System marks a great step forward in the computerization of Prudential's operations.

1975

The Bache Group is formed as a holding company. Bache Halsey Stuart becomes the principal operating unit.

With more than $200 billion in policies, Prudential becomes the company with the largest amount of insurance in force. It is now first in all three industry benchmarks—including total assets and annual premium income—laying undisputed claim to the title of the largest insurance company in the world.

Prudential incorporates its first HMO, PruCare, to operate in Houston.

1976

Forty-eight percent of Americans surveyed recall seeing an advertisement for Prudential in the past six months. Prudential advertises on such highly watched shows as "The Mary Tyler Moore Show," "M*A*S*H" and the "CBS Morning News."

As the nation celebrates its bicentennial, Prudential is a major corporate sponsor of the Freedom Train—a historical exhibit that travels through the country for nearly two years.

DONALD MACNAUGHTON (LEFT), ON THE FREEDOM TRAIN.

1977

The Prudential Foundation is established to administer the company's philanthropic activities.

The Bache Group acquires Shield Model Rolan. The name of the firm's chief brokerage and banking subsidiary is changed to Bache Halsey Stuart Shields Inc.

1983

The Bache Group acquires Harrison & Company. The firm also purchases a controlling interest in the Albert M. Bender Company, one of the largest private insurance brokerage firms in the Western United States. The Bache Group would acquire full ownership of the company in 1978.

Prudential replaces its famous "piece of the Rock" slogan with "They need me" and a focus on family.

CEO Donald S. MacNaughton helps raise $1 million for the John F. Kennedy Center for the Performing Arts in Washington, D.C.

1978

MacNaughton retires. Robert Beck is elected chairman and CEO.

1979

The Sony Prudential Life Insurance Company debuts in Japan as a joint effort between Sony and Prudential.

1980

Prudential gives $300,000 to Princeton University for the development of a thermal energy storage system, which uses pools of water to heat and cool buildings. The system is to be used in the building the company plans at Princeton's Forrestal Center.

PRUDENTIAL PRESIDENT DAVID SHERWOOD (LEFT), WITH A MODEL OF THE ENERPLEX COMPLEX, PRINCETON, NEW JERSEY.

The American Association for Retired Persons awards Prudential a health insurance contract. It is the largest new group case ever sold by an insurer.

Prudential begins offering lower rates for nonsmokers. The development of FOCUS—the Field Office Computerized Update System—improves processing and field office operations.

1981

Prudential acquires the securities brokerage firm of Bache Halsey Stuart Shields Inc. The firm is renamed Prudential-Bache Securities. It is Prudential's first major diversification beyond the insurance industry.

Prudential takes over the health insurance account of the National Retired Teachers Association—American Association of Retired Persons.

1982

Prudential sells the largest group creditors life insurance account in its history to the Oregon Department of Veterans Affairs. This account provides $3.7 billion of group credit coverage and annual premiums of $24 million.

In what might be the largest single real estate sale in the United States, Prudential assumes an 80 percent interest in Denver's City Center.

1983

Prudential acquires the Capital City Bank of Hapeville, Georgia. Its local assets are sold, and the bank is rechartered as the Prudential Bank and Trust Company.

Prudential reorganizes its U.S. insurance operations. Individual insurance is thereafter conducted through four rather than eight regional home offices. Group insurance works through five regional group offices, which are separate from the RHOs. Four RHOs remain: Fort Washington, Pennsylvania; Minneapolis, Minnesota; Los Angeles, California; and Jacksonville, Florida. About 1,700 jobs would be lost in this move. Regional offices in Boston, Massachusetts; Chicago, Illinois; Houston, Texas; and Woodbridge, New Jersey, would be converted to small group, property and casualty, and marketing operations.

An article in *Successful Farming* reports on the growing number of insurance companies buying farmland because it is proving to be a safe investment with good returns. The company with the largest holdings by far is Prudential. It has bought more than 750,000 acres, 85 percent of which were bought in the past three years.

1983

Prudential donates a 755-unit apartment complex to the New Community Corporation of Newark.

NEW COMMUNITY CORPORATION'S NEW APARTMENTS.

Prudential begins a program to hire back retirees as temporary employees.

The creation of Pru-MED signals Prudential's return to the individual health insurance market. Pru-MED would improve considerably on its predecessor's performance by encouraging more efficient, less costly use of medical care through features such as co-insurance and deductibles.

By June, more than half of Prudential's 22,000 agents have some form of securities licensing. By the end of the year, 30 Prudential locations are involved in joint brokerage-insurance operations.

1984

The company introduces the variable appreciable life policy. This new product offers customers a variety of ways to invest the cash value of their policies.

Prudential announces a reorganization of its investment organization.

Prudential begins studying demutualization.

Prudential donates 120,000 acres of prime wetlands to the U.S. Fish and Wildlife Service for a nature reserve. At the time, it is the largest contribution of private land for conservancy in the nation's history.

Prudential begins negotiating with the Newark Board of Education to sell the Gibraltar Building to the city.

Prudential announces that its health insurance plans will now cover heart and liver transplants.

Prudential ends its policy of supplying free lunches to employees.

Three Executive Office positions of equal rank are created, and Robert C. Winters becomes vice chairman for central corporate operations.

The Prudential Bank markets its first product, home equity loans, through Pru-Bache advisers.

1985

Assets surpass $100 billion.

The company acquires the Jennison Associates Capital Corporation, a stock and bond manager of pension funds.

Prudential's variable appreciable life policy becomes its most popular life insurance policy because it blends premium payment flexibility with guaranteed lifetime protection.

The Prudential Home Mortgage Company enables Prudential to re-enter the residential mortgage market after a 20-year absence.

1986

Prudential establishes The Prudential Dental Maintenance Organization, the first national managed dental care program. A retail branch of Prudential-Bache in Atlanta becomes the first securities office in the world to use satellite transmission to communicate with the floor of the New York Stock Exchange.

Prudential finances an $800 million mortgage loan for R.H. Macy & Company in conjunction with a leveraged buyout.

1987

Beck retires, and Robert C. Winters becomes Prudential's chairman and CEO.

WINTERS, WITH PRESIDENT
GEORGE BUSH.

The company forms a new subsidiary, Prudential Real Estate Affiliates, its first venture into the residential real estate brokerage business.

Prudential establishes Prudential Mutual Fund Management to administer the company's growing family of mutual funds. Prudential-Bache Securities acquires Thomson McKinnon Securities, increasing Prudential-Bache's sales force by 30 percent and making it the third-largest brokerage concern in the United States.

The Prudential Bank and Trust Company begins offering home equity loans in 32 states.

Prudential-Bache Securities incurs a $164 million loss partially because of the October stock market crash.

The Prudential Dental Maintenance Organization enrolls its millionth member.

After signing an agreement with Signet Bank of Virginia, the company begins to issue credit cards and process accounts for the new Prudential MasterCard.

Prudential Bank's assets surpass $100 million.

1988

All new Prudential agents must be licensed in all major product lines, including variable contracts and mutual funds.

Prudential Life Insurance Company Ltd. Japan establishes 10 new agencies.

Prudential terminates its services as a federal Medicare contractor.

1989

The Prudential "Rock" changes from an abstract form back to a more traditional appearance.

Prudential joins the Robert Wood Johnson Foundation in a new program that develops mental health services for children and adolescents.

Prudential acquires the Cartersville Federal Savings and Loan Association. It is renamed the Prudential Savings Bank.

Prudential surpasses $200 billion in assets under management.

1990

The company begins selling insurance in Spain, Italy and Taiwan.

Prudential establishes an office in Tokyo to manage global securities for Japanese clients.

Prudential introduces the Living Needs Benefit program in the United States. It enables the terminally ill or those permanently confined to a nursing home to collect life insurance benefits while they are still living. Jan Anderson and her family become the first recipients when her husband becomes terminally ill.

1990

The Prudential Global Real Estate Investment Programme, a $2 billion partnership between Prudential and Jones Lang Wootten, a British real estate advisory firm, is created. The program is intended to help clients build a global real estate portfolio.

Prudential Bank's credit card operations are brought in-house. Prudential begins to offer VISA credit cards.

1991

Prudential begins sales in South Korea.

Prudential-Bache Securities changes its name to Prudential Securities.

The Prudential Foundation donates $200,000 to the Vietnam Veterans Memorial Fund for the addition of names to and the upkeep of the Vietnam Veterans Memorial in Washington, D.C.

The foundation also launches the Focus on Children program, which provides more than $1 million in grants to improve the lives of preschool children.

Prudential Securities rebounds from 1990, increasing earnings by $460 million.

PRUPAC's losses exceed $40 million in the second-worst catastrophe year on record.

The Prudential Bank introduces the Prudential Business Card and begins offering certificates of deposit through Prudential Securities advisers.

Prudential purchases $150 million in home equity loans from Shearson Mortgage.

VIETNAM VETERANS MEMORIAL, 1991.

1992

Prudential President Ronald D. Barbaro retires.

BARBARO, WITH GOV. MARIO CUOMO.

Prudential unveils "Community Champions," a companywide employee volunteer recognition program.

The Living Needs Benefit program reaches all 50 states. New York is the last to approve it.

In the wake of Hurricane Andrew, Prudential pays out $1.5 billion in claims.

1993

Prudential establishes its Community Action Relief Effort, or the Prudential CARES program. Thousands of Prudential employees donate money to hurricane and flood victims.

Prudential Securities agrees to settle legal claims. Investors from throughout the United States had charged the company with investment fraud.

Prudential surpasses $250 billion in assets under management.

1994

Robert Winters retires, and Arthur F. Ryan becomes Prudential's chairman and CEO.

ARTHUR F. RYAN.

Prudential launches the Helping Hearts program in New Jersey. The company pledges $150,000 every three years to purchase defibrillators for local volunteer first-aid squads.

DONATION BY HELPING HEARTS.

Prudential's capital declines 11 percent in one of the most difficult years in its history.

Prudential Securities resolves limited partnership problems dating back to the 1980s.

Claims are paid to policyholders in connection with a California earthquake and severe storms in the Northeast.

1995

Fortune magazine adds Prudential to its list of top 500 companies. It ranks 5th in total assets, 13th in revenue and 37th in the number of employees.

Prudential announces plans to sell its home mortgage business and its Prudential Reinsurance Holdings unit.

Prudential forms the Money Management Group to offer more savings and investment products.

Prudential Bank launches a co-branded VISA card with BellSouth.

Prudential is awarded the U.S. Department of the Treasury Award for its support of the U.S. Savings Bond Program.

Prudential is selected as one of nine companies to participate in the Federal Diversity Benchmarking Study, part of Vice President Al Gore's National Partnership for Reinventing Government.

1996

1996

The Prudential Foundation donates $1.5 million to the Newark school district.

The American Association of Retired Persons decides not to renew its $4 billion health insurance contract with Prudential.

Prudential is fined $35 million for deceptive life insurance sales practices going back to 1982.

Prudential launches its "One Prudential" initiative, an effort to break down the barriers among the various components of Prudential's business.

As part of One Prudential, the company chooses Minneapolis, Phoenix and Richmond as test cities where customers are able to access numerous Prudential services and resources in one central location.

The number of processing locations for Prudential HealthCare Operations and Systems is reduced from 46 to 4.

Prudential receives the National Points of Light Foundation Award for Excellence in Corporate Community Service and the Child Welfare League of America Corporate Advocate of the Year award.

1997

Prudential settles a nationwide class-action lawsuit, agreeing to pay $400 million to customers.

Prudential puts three pieces of Manhattan real estate on the market, thereby bowing out of the Times Square urban renewal project, with which it had been involved since the mid-1980s.

Prudential begins to do business in Latin America, entering into a joint venture with Bradesco Seguros, a subsidiary of Brazil's largest bank.

The Prudential Foundation commits $6.5 million toward the New Jersey Performing Arts Center. Prudential is the largest single corporate benefactor.

NJPAC BUILDING.

Prudential begins selling off its credit card portfolios.

Prudential surpasses $300 billion in assets under management.

1998

Governor Christine Whitman signs the New Jersey Demutualization Bill in July.

Prudential announces that it is looking at the process of demutualization.

Prudential announces its plans to sell its health insurance operations to the Aetna Insurance Company.

Prudential receives the President's Service Award from the Points of Light Foundation.

Prudential Retirement Services wins Microsoft's Windows World Open award for the development of its Common Front End system.

1999

Prudential announces the formation of Prudential Seguros S.A., its life insurance affiliate in Buenos Aires.

The company opens a life insurance affiliate in Poland, which uses Prudential's new international brand—Prumerica.

Pricoa Vita S.P.A., Prudential's Italian life insurance affiliate, changes its name to Prumerica Life S.P.A.

Prudential begins selling life insurance in the Philippines.

Prudential is named to *Working Mother* magazine's list of top 10 companies for working mothers after making the publication's top 100 list nine times since 1987.

Prudential enters the long-term care market.

Prudential offers auto rate quotes via its Web site.

Prudential Filipino insurance operations begin to sell products under the company's international brand.

PruTector becomes available in Florida.

Prudential expands its presence in Japan by entering the pension fund business.

Prudential Health Care is sold to Aetna.

Prudential kicks off its yearlong 125th anniversary celebration October 2 with its Fifth Annual Global Volunteer Day. Prudential volunteers contribute more than 95,000 hours of volunteer service.

Prudential makes *Information Week*'s top 100 e-businesses list, ranking 36th.

Prudential agrees to acquire Apolo Operadora de Sociedades de Inversion S.A. de C.V., a Mexican investment management company. The acquisition forms Prudential Apolo Operadora de Sociedades de Inversion S.A. de C.V.

Prudential acquires Hochman and Baker Inc., a firm that recruits and trains accounting professionals to become licensed to offer investment and insurance products to their tax and business clients. Prudential then adds certified public accountants as a distribution channel for its investment and insurance products.

2000

Black Collegian magazine names Prudential to its top 100 employers of entry-level 1999 college graduates.

Working Women magazine names Prudential among its top 25 companies in the United States for executive women.

Prudential acquires St. Paul Specialty Auto, enhancing the company's property and casualty business through its entry into the fast-growing nonstandard auto insurance market.

PAT RYAN "DIGS IN" ON GLOBAL VOLUNTEER DAY.

Getting the Word Out

Life Insurance —
a bond of esteem
and affection

THE PRUDENTIAL
HAS THE
STRENGTH OF
GIBRALTAR

THE PRUDENTIAL INSURANCE COMPANY
OF AMERICA

Home Office, NEWARK, NEW JERSEY

In colonial America, newspapers and broadsheets advertised newly available goods and services or announced that a valuable piece of cargo was about to arrive in port. Over the next 300 years, American advertising would change in both form and function, evolving into a device of such pervasiveness and sophistication that it could—and did—change the way we think and behave.

Early Americans were peppered with ads offering some version of "snake oil" or get-rich-quick schemes. After the Civil War, industrialization accelerated, and industrial barons saw advertising as a necessary defense against the competition. The first widespread use of recognizable *trademarks helped to establish products' legitimacy.*

Competition increased as companies found ways to produce goods in large numbers and with greater efficiency. In the first half of the 20th century, advertising became an even more necessary element of commerce, differentiating products, creating brand loyalty and motivating consumers.

The Prudential Insurance Company of America began to advertise soon after it opened

OPPOSITE: CALENDAR, 1899. BELOW (FROM LEFT): CALENDARS, 1905, 1917 AND 1923.

OPPOSITE: PRINT AD, 1918. *ABOVE (CLOCKWISE):* PIN TRAY, MATCHBOOK, PIN CUSHION, THIMBLE AND PIN.

its doors in 1875. The company's earliest ads were simple newspaper testimonials extolling the benefits of industrial insurance, a form of life insurance that Prudential was the first to offer to working-class Americans. As the practice of advertising as a whole became more sophisticated, so did Prudential's, most profoundly so in its 1896 advertisement in Leslie's Weekly *that claimed, beneath the now-famous landscape,* "The Prudential Has the Strength of Gibraltar." *In the span of a line, one of advertising's most enduring icons was born.*

1875

1896

1904

1906

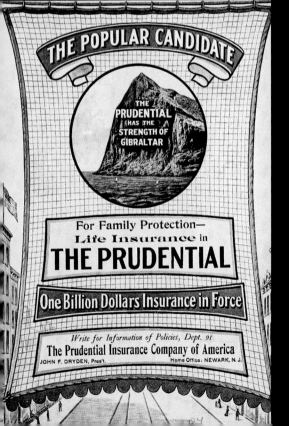
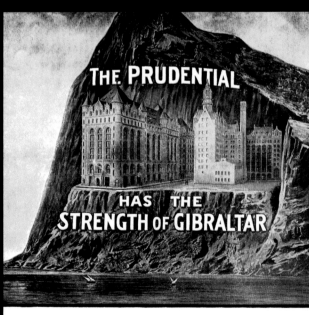

1918

1919

1924

1926

May They Never Be In Want

ADEQUATE PROTECTION FOR <u>YOUR</u> <u>LOVED</u> ONES
<u>ASSURED</u> BY

THE PRUDENTIAL INSURANCE COMPANY OF AMERIC

EDWARD D. DUFFIELD, *President*

HOME OFFICE, *Newark, N. J*

With the dawn of radio and television, Prudential's advertising evolved to reach an increasingly affluent American market. Its lessons on the necessity of insurance and family-based financial planning were aired on Prudential-sponsored programs of the 1950s, such as the "Prudential Family Hour" and the "Jack Berch

OPPOSITE: PRINT AD, 1933. *BELOW (FROM LEFT):* PRINT ADS, 1944 AND 1952.

The girl who is pledged to Humanity

I know that on every battlefront some woman—such as I shall try to be—is helping to save the lives of American soldiers, perhaps the life of my own brother, perhaps your sweetheart.

Nurses are needed everywhere, and so I am going to be a nurse . . . training here at home . . . with later a free choice of how I shall serve. I am going to help people get well, and someday I am going to be a better wife and mother, too, because of this training in the proud profession of nursing.

Yes, nurses are needed—here at home in *civilian* hospitals and clinics as well as military. To train them, your government, through the U. S. Cadet Nurse Corps, offers to intelligent young women a professional education *free* . . .

with smart street uniforms . . . a monthly allowance w learning . . . preparation for a wide choice of interesting w such as nursing executive, public health nurse, child he specialist, or anesthetist. And *in any essential nursing job,* will be serving your country as well as yourself. If you a high-school graduate, between 17 and 35, with a good sc lastic record, and in good health, get further informa now at the nearest hospital, or write: U. S. Cadet N Corps (U.S. Public Health Service), Box 88, New York, N

THIS MESSAGE CONTRIBUTED BY

THE PRUDENTIAL
INSURANCE COMPANY OF AMERICA
A mutual life insurance company
HOME OFFICE: NEWARK, NEW JERSEY

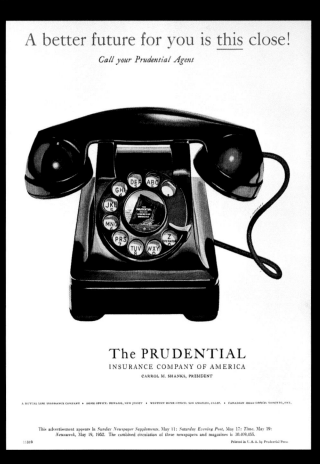

A better future for you is <u>this</u> close!

Call your Prudential Agent

The PRUDENTIAL
INSURANCE COMPANY OF AMERICA
CARROL M. SHANKS, PRESIDENT

A MUTUAL LIFE INSURANCE COMPANY • HOME OFFICE: NEWARK, NEW JERSEY • WESTERN HOME OFFICE: LOS ANGELES, CALIF. • CANADIAN HEAD OFFICE: TORONTO, ONT.

This advertisement appears in *Sunday Newspaper Supplements,* May 11: *Saturday Evening Post,* May 17; *Time,* May 19; *Newsweek,* May 19, 1952. The combined circulation of these newspapers and magazines is 30,400,455.

Printed in U.S.A. by Prudential Press

Pick out your neighbor

These seven men illustrate something the Prudential believes is important: you serve people best as a neighbor. That's why we've built a series of Home Offices across the nation — to be closer to you... to give you swifter and better insurance service. To be, in short, a real neighbor. *See your Prudential Agent.*

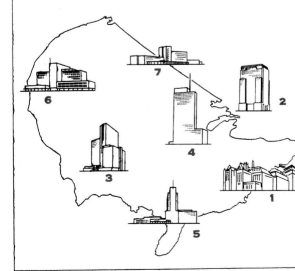

1 NEWARK · NEW JERSEY   2 TORONTO · CANADA   3 HOUSTON · TEXAS   4 CHICAGO · ILLINOIS
5 JACKSONVILLE · FLORIDA   6 LOS ANGELES · CALIFORNIA   7 MINNEAPOLIS · MINNESOTA

Show." The slogan, "Get a piece of the Rock," became an American icon.

Today, Prudential is venturing into cyberspace as e-commerce brings vast changes to the world's buying habits. Yet, the image of "the Rock"—like Prudential itself—endures.

OPPOSITE: PRINT AD, 1955. BELOW (FROM LEFT): PRINT ADS, 1965 AND 1971.

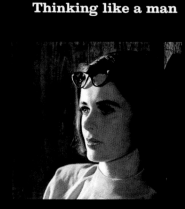

Thinking like a man

No job for a woman.
No job for your wife—taking care of things that should not be her responsibility alone.
Things like the mortgage. And the kids' college. And how to live—comfortably

—if you're not around.
That's *your* job. But don't try to do it by yourself. Use your Prudential "pro". He can translate those figures in your insurance policy into what really counts: *the continuing security that Income*

Dollars bring . . . to feed your family . . . and clothe them . . . and house them . . . and educate them—year-in, year-out. And he brings you the best references in the world: from millions of policyholders.

THE PRUDENTIAL INSURANCE COMPANY OF AMERICA

PRU-744
This advertisement prepared by:
REACH McCLINTON & CO., INC.
to appear in:
Life—March 5, 1965
1 Page—4 Color

"It came with my piece of the Rock."

"While my policy helps protect my income, some of my premiums are invested in the Empire State!"

That's right, the Empire State. Because he got a piece of the Rock along with his Prudential Income Protection Policy. Owning a piece of the Rock means we make investments

with his premiums—in real estate, among other things. Investments that strengthen the economy and can help pay dividends to keep his insurance costs down. This young man's insurance can help protect his income when he's unable to work due to sickness or injury.

Ask a Prudential agent what proper income protection can mean to your financial security.
Ask him about building it on a piece of the Rock.

Prudential
Health Insurance

Index

Acknowledgments

The task of including every significant and important fact in this 125th anniversary book is difficult enough. Giving proper recognition to every individual who helped produce the book is an impossible chore—we would have to include not just each employee who has ever worked for Prudential but certainly we would honor every policyholder who placed his or her faith and trust in our company.

For the sake of space, we have to limit our acknowledgments to those who have gone above and beyond the call of duty in developing this bound testament to the valuable work of Pru People past and present, making Prudential the "Rock" that it is today.

We thank all those who contributed their time and creative energy, and more than a few overtime hours in pulling together elements of this book from—literally—around the world. Those people include: Debra Abeigon, Christine Ahn, Suneet Bhatt, Carolyn Brooks, Gordon Calder, George Cook, John Cooke, Bob DeFillippo, Rene Deida, Jason Dressel, Paul Freer, Tonya Handford, Evelyn Lesnik, Leonard Lesnik, Cathy Looney, Kevin Manzel, Mary O'Malley, Glenn Nutting, Juliana Pereira, Maureen Schmidt, Christina Simms, Cathy Szillage-Looney, Connie Wilson, Dorothy Wolfe, and Dr. Terrence P. Zealand, Ed.D.

We thank Pat Ryan for providing her tireless spirit and energy to make the dream of a 125th anniversary book a reality. Logging thousands of frequent-flier miles, Pat Ryan personally led the effort to oversee and gather the employee stories that are featured in the section "Toward a New Century—Stories of Prudential and Its People."

We thank the many Prudential employees who offered their personal experiences to this book and, thus, to Prudential's permanent historical record. These generous individuals include:

Larry Andrews

Mario Acquista

Denny Axman

Marty Berkowitz

Terry Brehony

Patricia Brzozowski

Weon Il Choi

George Coleman

Louise Cook

Gail Crawford

Gerald Deridder

Ray Dewey

Mack Garrett

Joe Garza

Jimmie Gonzalez

Victor Howard

Marcel Idiart

Gerald Kuschuk

Ina Liss

Bella Loykhter

Angie Mann

Takashi Matsumoto

Merle Mattenson

Sherry Meier

Brian Murphy

Tomomi Nishikawa

Mary O'Malley

Bruno Pinkos

Thom Powers

Ray Ranucci

Joe Ritchie

Bob Satterfield

Fred Schubert

Donna Strohm

Darcy Todia

Denis Underkoffler

Naoko Watanabe

Carol Whitesell

Dorothy Wolfe

Yvonne Yamatani

Rosalee Zodikoff

Photo Credits

For more than one picture on a page, credits read clockwise from top left unless noted.

FOREWORD: 6: Prudential Archives **7:** Allan Hunter Shoemake **A CORPORATION ASKS, WHO AM I?: 10-12:** (all) Prudential Archives **13:** Frank DiGiacomo/*The Star-Ledger*; Nooney Ritacco; Prudential Archives **14:** Prudential Archives; George Van Photographer/Prudential Archives **15:** (all) Prudential Archives **16:** Courtesy of Michael Mattia/Prudential Archives; J. Eickenbush Photographer/Prudential Archives; Prudential Archives **17:** Prudential Archives **18:** Handy & Boesser Photographers, Newark/Prudential Archives; Prudential Archives **19:** George Andrews/*The Star-Ledger*. **BUILDING A FOUNDATION: 23-26:** (all) Prudential Archives **27:** Empire Art Studio, New York/Prudential Archives **28-29:** (both) Prudential Archives **30:** *Newark Star*/Prudential Archives **31-33:** (both) Prudential Archives **34:** Keystone View Co. Inc. of N.Y./Prudential Archives **35-36:** (both) Prudential Archives **37:** Corbis/International News Photos © **38:** Photo by Gerry Billard for Ken Bell Photography, Toronto, Ontario/Prudential Archives **39:** Prudential Archives **40:** Al Howard, Chicago/Prudential Archives **41:** Ralph Morse/TimePix **42:** Jax Camera Center/Prudential Archives **43:** Elliott G. Smith, Jr./Prudential Archives **44:** Bodden Fotos/Prudential Archives **45:** Jax Camera Center/Prudential Archives **46:** Prudential Archives **47:** Commercial Photographic Company, Inc./Prudential Archives **48:** Fay Foto Service, Inc./Prudential Archives **49:** Prudential Archives **50-51:** (both) Armen Photographers/Prudential Archives. **TRAGEDY AND TRIUMPH: 52-53:** Chicago Historical Society/ICHi-02036 **54:** Prudential Archives **55:** Library of Congress, Prints and Photographs Division [LC-USZ62-95096]; Prudential Archives **56-57:** (all) Prudential Archives **58-59:** Prudential Archives; J.A. Van Roden, Newark, NJ/Prudential Archives **60:** Amanda Brown/*The Star-Ledger*; (all) Prudential Archives **61:** Prudential Archives. **TOWARD A NEW CENTURY: 65:** Prudential Archives **66-67:** (both) Rogerio Reis/Black Star **68-69:** (both) Prudential Archives **71-73:** (all) Prudential Archives **74:** Handy & Boesser Photographers/Prudential Archives **75:** *The Star-Ledger*/Prudential Archives; Camera Arts Studio/Prudential Archives **76-81:** (all) Prudential Archives **82:** City of Toronto Archives **83:** From the collection of the Maritime Museum of the Atlantic, Halifax, Nova Scotia, CANADA **84-85:** (both) Prudential Archives **86:** Robert Sciarrino/*The Star-Ledger* **87:** Richard Chu/*The Star-Ledger* **88-89:** (both) Prudential Archives **90:** Chicago Historical Society, ICHi-26695/*Chicago Daily News* **91:** Chicago Historical Society, ICHi-26980/*Chicago Daily News* **92:** Bruce Wodder **93:** Prudential Archives **94:** Richard Rosenberg/*The Star-Ledger* **95-99:** (all) Prudential Archives **101:** Used with permission from the Rough Notes Co., Indianapolis, Indiana/Prudential Archives **102:** Prudential Archives **103:** U.S. Army Signal Corps Photo/Prudential Archives **104-105:** (both) Courtesy The Newark Public Library/Prudential Archives **106-107:** (both) Prudential Archives **108:** P. Sclarandis/Black Star **109:** Courtesy of Dr. Terrence P. Zealand **110-112:** (all) Prudential Archives **113:** William D. Clare/Prudential Archives **114:** AP/Wide World Photos **115:** *Puck*, August 2, 1905 **116-118:** (all) Prudential Archives **119:** AP/National Museum of Health and Medicine **120:** Prudential Archives **121:** Global Photo Assignments **123-124:** (both) Prudential Archives **125:** Citywide Corporate Photography **126:** Prudential Archives **127:** Jax Camera Center/Prudential Archives; Prudential Archives **129-131:** (all) Prudential Archives **132:** Courtesy of Leonard and Evelyn Lesnik **133:** (both) Prudential Archives **134:** Glenn Nutting **135-139:** (all) Prudential Archives **140:** AP/Wide World Photos **141:** Ki Ho Park/Global Photo Assignments **142-143:** (both) Courtesy of Darcy Todia **144-149:** (all) Prudential Archives **150:** Vic Yepello/*The Star-Ledger* **151:** Cheryl Sheridan/Black Star **152:** Copyright *TIME* Magazine **153:** Duval Commercial Photographers/Prudential Archives **155:** Bodden Fotos/Prudential Archives **156-157:** (both) Citywide Corporate Photography. **WOMEN IN THE WORKPLACE: 158-159:** Bodden Fotos/Prudential Archives **160-165:** (all) Prudential Archives **166:** Prudential Archives; Prudential Archives; Citywide Corporate Photography **167:** Prudential Archives. **CHARTING THE ROCK'S COURSE: 170-177:** (all) Prudential Archives **178:** Bob Bailey Fine Photography/Prudential Archives **179:** Used with permission from Walter Cronkite/CBS Photo Archive; (both) Prudential Archives **180:** (both) Prudential Archives **181:** Frank DiGiacomo/*The Star-Ledger*; Prudential Archives **182:** (both) Prudential Archives **183:** Edward Stiso/*The Star-Ledger* **184:** Mark Abraham/*The Star-Ledger* **185:** Courtesy of the Prudential Public Relations Department **186-187:** (all) Prudential Archives **188:** Dario Acosta **189:** Samir Id-Deen/*The Star-Ledger*. **GETTING THE WORD OUT: 190-201:** (all) Prudential Archives

Winners of the Chairman's Award for Excellence in Innovation

LaunchPad
Renee Artiges
Maurice L. Bellfield
Stephen R. Brotz
Michael Cloutier
Maynard O. Crawley
Robert P. Davies
Mary Rose Freddo
Kurt Gillhaus
Patricia A. Greenwood
Barbara L. Halaburda
Sol Hicks
Ari D. Horowitz
Zahra Jafar
William K. Kehoe
David A. Kindt
Christine R. Ludwig
Jerry R. Mac Lean
Ida R. Machuca
Anthony R. Melchione
Shawn A. Murray
Bernard M. O'Neill
Jeffrey L. Olson
Lisa A. Otto
Frank R. Perri
Robert C. Piccirillo
Fred K. Prasse
Gregory J. Schmitt
Roy J. Schwartz
Michael Scoda
Michael Shapiro
Alfred P. Spangenberg
William R. Tranter
Donna M. Vecchiarelli
Denise E. Weiner
Albert W. Wolff

PRUCRU
Philip Augello
Joseph J. Baron
Glenn A. Basko
Thomas E. Conner
Donald J. DeFalco
Gustavo B. Garguillo
Laura A. Gashlin
William M. Gaydos
Robert J. Hayes
Joann K. Heinle

John A. Jackson
Mark J. McVey
Susan M. Morales
Dominick Romano
Ronald Sorenson
Robert R. Way
Philip M. Wegelin
Thomas S. Widelski
Dean Winitt

Living Needs Benefit
Nancy Baran
Helen M. Galt
Eleanor S. Hartley
Robert Hill
Richard E. Meade
Walter Miller
Paul Nolle
James M. O'Connor
Kieran J. Quinn

Individual Long Term Care
Angela M. Bresadola
Gail E. Holubinka
Denise La Capra
Joseph D. Schroeder
Stephen P. Shea
Karen L. Smyth

Individual Winner
Constance O. Garretson
Minority Interchange, Inc.

PruServ
John G. Alouisa
Andrew G. Blackwood
Yisroel Y. Bongart
William J. Carroll
Salvatore Coco
Harvey I. Cohen
Brett C. Doty
Barbara Dreyfus
Raymond S. Ennis
Lillian J. Escobar-Diaz

Paul M. Goldsmith
Nicole A. Hall
Julia A. Herbert
Carol L. Karwacki
Kevin G. Kennedy
James A. Lambiase
Joseph Luino
Michael G. Maloney
Andrew P. McAllister
Christine T. McDermott
John C. McHugh
Leah S. Nebenzahl
Russell Pandolfo
Barbara Puccia
Abbe L. Rosenbaum
Laibe Schwartz
David Tovey
LaVern L. Walsh

The Prudential Spirit of Community Awards
Jamie R. Chasinov
Robert P. Fallon
Alan K. Glover
Patricia A. Krietzberg
Scott H. Peterson
Sylvia Rosado

Individual Winner
Joseph F. Dunn
Prudential of Japan Model

Prudential Advisor
Andrew Alexopoulos
John G. Alouisa
Joseph L. Alzza
Robert Anselmo
Morris E. Brown
Susan T. Carragher
Salvatore Coco
Megan C. Demonte
Stuart M. Feld
Joseph A. Garritano
Vincent A. Giampapa
Kipp Good
Elliot Goryachkovsky

Elisabeth C. Gougelmann
Robert J. Hanna
Kevin G. Kennedy
Richard P. Kovitch
Peter Kui
Andrew J. Lippman
Steven P. Little
Richard Mason
Andrew P. McAllister
Maribeth H. Molina
Anthony Muzio
Gregg S. Pearlstein
Valentin J. Tellado
Daniel S. Valentino
Robert J. Walsh
Susan Wu

Project Transformation
Joseph Calello
Sharon Barnes
Bernard Buchholz
Paul Egan
Robert Falzon
Allen Green
John Gregorits
John Kelly
Joseph Margolis
James W. McCarthy
Kurt Metzger
Harry Mixon
Brian Murphy
Allen Ostroff
Stephen Parker
Eileen Power
David A. Twardock
Steven Vittorio
Ralph Wheatly
Bernard Winograd
Cher Zucker-Maltese

The Chairman's Award for Excellence In Innovation

Recognizing the creative spirit and achievement that defines Prudential. This Award commemorates the company's most notable gains of the past 25 years— and the visionary and creative Prudential people who have made them happen.

PruServ Team

Gail E. Holubinka— Individual Long Term Care Team Member

Project Transformation Team

Accepting for Constance O. Garretson, Teresa Warren

Roy J. Schwartz— LaunchPad Team Member

Living Needs Benefit Team

Prudential Financial